Coping WITH SCHOOL

Peter Corey

- illustrated by -
Martin BROWN

Hippo

D0552285

Scholastic Children's Books,
Commonwealth House, 1-19 New Oxford Street,
London, WC1A 1NU, UK
a division of Scholastic Publications Ltd
London ~ New York ~ Toronto ~ Sydney ~ Auckland

First published in the UK by Scholastic Ltd, 1994

Text copyright © Peter Corey, 1993
Illustrations © Martin Brown, 1993

ISBN: 0 590 55279 1

All rights reserved
Printed by Cox & Wyman, Reading, Berks
Typeset by Goodfellow & Egan

10 9 8 7 6

The right of Peter Corey and Martin Brown to be identified as the author and illustrator
respectively of this work has been asserted by them in accordance with the
Copyright, Designs and Patents Act, 1988.

This book is sold subject to the condition that it shall not, by way of trade or otherwise, be lent,
resold, hired out, or otherwise circulated without the publisher's prior consent in any form of
binding or cover other than that in which it is published and without a similar condition,
including this condition, being imposed upon the subsequent purchaser.

Contents...

Dedication...

This book is dedicated to Micky Shorthouse.

The only way to survive school is to have a really good friend to help you through the tough times, let you copy their homework, do your lines for you, and disguise themselves as you on sports day so that you don't actually have to run the 100-metres (which you've been roped into against your will and medical advice, but which the whole of your school house is banking on you winning because they stand to lose *thousands* if you don't).

Micky Shorthouse did none of these things. But he was still the best mate anyone could have. In fact, our friendship ran so deep that from the day we left school to the present time, we haven't contacted each other once.

School can do that to you!

MICKY SHORTHOUSE AGE 12 TAKEN BY ME

Foreword

Coping With School? But haven't we already had *Coping With Teachers*? Ah, yes, we have. And those of you who have read it will realize that it deals with a very specific area of school life, namely teachers, which goes some way to explaining that particular book's carefully chosen title. Incidentally, if you haven't read it, it's probably because you haven't got a copy. So I suggest you go and get one right now. I don't mind waiting. Right. Got it? Now read it. Quicker than that! Right. Finished? Good, isn't it? But, brilliant though it may be, it only deals with the tip of the iceberg. Oh, yes! There's far more to school than teachers, just as there's far more to train-spotting than standing around looking a dinkle in a plastic mac.

School is an intricate topic. Let's face it, anything that involves taking a packed lunch has got to be complex.[1] School is the one place we all have to go to. Without a trial and with no chance of appeal, we get banged up for at least twelve years – longer in some cases. As for teachers, they get a life sentence without time off for good behaviour (unless of course you count those long holidays)!

Because school is something we can't avoid, we need help to cope with the situation. And that's what this book is all about. It will answer all your questions, even the ones you'd never thought of asking. So dive in! Your education starts here!

---

1. See section on school dinners.

Acknowledgements

Naturally I realize that I couldn't possibly tackle a task as mammoth as this book proved to be, without surrounding myself with a team of experts. And that's exactly what I did. The experts were hand-picked, not to say hand-cuffed, until the task was finished. They were:

Elderado Dingbatti

No stranger to research projects such as this, he is also no stranger to the insides of institutions catering specifically for people who believe themselves to be somebody or something else. Elderado currently believes himself to be a TV soap opera. There was of course a BBC TV soap opera called *Eldorado*, which owed its "success" to the winning combination of Sun, Sand and Really Bad Acting[1]. It is now gone but not forgotten.[2] Anyway, no amount of pointing out to Elderado Dingbatti that *Eldorado* was spelt differently, and was even more boring than he is, makes any difference. He is totally convinced that he will suffer the same fate

1. Hard to believe it wasn't a success; after all, the same combination works for *Home and Away*.
2. There are still people working at the BBC who shudder at the mention of it!

9

as his soap opera namesake. Namely, that no-one will take any notice of him and eventually he'll be killed off. The plus side of this condition is that, rather like the soap opera, I only had to put up with seeing him three times a week for half an hour[1]. And he did come up with some useful, if bizarre, information – as you will probably see from this book.

Lauden Forthright BA, BSc, MFI

An ex-headmaster, Lauden was an obvious choice for my research team, although I have to say that I didn't actually select him. He selected himself, and threatened to keep me in if I didn't agree. A headmaster of the old school, he took early retirement when his school governors abolished hanging as a fit punishment for forgetting your gym kit. He then took a job as an ice-cream seller, but frightened so many of his customers by asking – in a voice than could shatter glass – if they wanted a 99 or crushed nuts, that the ice-cream firm went out of business. However, I have to admit that he was very helpful

---

1. Although – again rather like the soap opera – he did pop round on a couple of other occasions, but only to repeat everything he'd already told me.

with some of the more obscure school regulations, as long as I kept him sedated.

Miss Prim

Who isn't at all as her name suggests. In fact, she's the size of a carthorse and smells of lavender. But her heart is in the right place, presumably. It's hard to tell under all those layers of hand-knitted sensible clothing. It is rumoured that once, when she was teaching at the Bumpy Road Mixed Infants School in Chester-le-Street, one of her pupils disappeared for a week. He was found alive, well and extremely warm, in the folds of her cardigan. Apparently he had survived by nibbling on a family-size egg custard that had gone missing a couple of days earlier. The most extraordinary thing about this story is that the little boy's parents didn't miss him. Some kids have all the luck, eh? Miss Prim was extremely useful for keeping us all going, especially with her home-made treacle tart. Her only fault was that she kept stopping us working so that we could have recorder practice.

A.J. Gruntwick
(RN Retired)

Since this book is not only about education but also about the broader topic of school, I decided that it would be a good idea to have a school caretaker on my team. It wasn't. It was a terrible idea. It was probably about the worst idea I've ever had.[1] It wasn't until after I had negotiated a ridiculously large sum of money[2] for his services that I realized there is only ever one reason why anyone becomes a school caretaker: *revenge!*

1. That is, if you don't count the idea I once had to attempt the first Alpine crossing in a canoe. It wasn't until I was about to set off that someone pointed out that the Alps were mountains. I didn't realize this, having been away from school when they did geography.
2. Ridiculously large by my standards, that is. Almost running into double figures.

These were the experts, although I feel a word of thanks is due to Mrs Jaffa, School Secretary of the Jason Donovan County Secondary School in Wisbech. And to Miss Padgett for correcting the spelling, although I personally don't believe that it was totally necessary for her to insist that I write out five million times: *I must get at least a modest grasp of basic punctuation.* There are others, of course, without whom etc., etc., but they are too numerous to mention. They are also the kind of people who will want a cut of the profits if they see their names in print.

My sincerest thanks go out to all of them, and we'll say no more about the incident with the hamster and the rubber bands.

Peter Corey, Dungeness Power Station[1]

1. I'm not actually anywhere near Dungeness Power Station, but I've noticed in other books how writers put an exotic place after their name, to make you think that they're on holiday or a tax exile or something. So I thought I'd do the same. Dungeness may not be exotic, but it's certainly unusual.

A potted history of school

Then the whining schoolboy, with his satchel and shining morning face creeping like a snail unwillingly to school

I think that Shakespeare quote more or less says it all. Nobody likes school. Now, that may seem like an outrageous statement, but it's true. OK, so there might be bits of school life that individuals like, such as home time, or playtime. Some people might even like some of the lessons. Some of the teachers teaching the lessons might even quite like them. But no-one can honestly say that they like school, without reservation. Unless they're mad, in which case they probably like all sorts of weird things, like Jeremy Beadle and Timmy Mallet. So, if school is such an awful place, what kind of idiot thought it up? To discover that, we have to dig deep in the sands of time, turn back the pages of history, and then quickly run out of clichés. . .

At the dawn of time, when dinosaurs roamed the Earth, there was man.[1] Man had been roaming the Earth, but had now got thoroughly fed up with it. The Earth at that point was mostly swamp, and it didn't take a brain the

1. OK, I know man wasn't around at the time of the dinosaurs, but it's more fun if we pretend he was!

14

size of Manchester to realize that swamp is a lot easier to sink into than walk on. It also played havoc with your socks. Well, when I say socks, imagine bits of Nodosaurus[1] intestine strapped to your feet. Not much of a fashion statement, but at least they kept out the swamp. Shoes hadn't been invented, obviously. *Travel Fox* were very much a thing of the future.

1. At least it would have been Nodosaurus in North America. The poor old primitive Britons would have had to settle for Bary Onyx, which is a lot less *Airwear* and a lot more *Freeman, Hardy and Willis*.

So primitive man found himself a cave, scribbed *Dunroamin* over the entrance in berry-juice, and settled down. And there he would have stayed until, just like the dinosaur, progress overtook him or the swamp got to him, and he became extinct. But he didn't. One day, probably a Thursday, one particular primitive man (we'll call him Lionel)[1] had just stuck his pointed stick into a lump of Acanthopolis, and a great squirt of grease had gone down the lapel of his Hyleasaurus casuals.[2] Lionel looked at his lapel and grunted.[3] He had a heavy date later that afternoon – a real beauty who'd just moved into the cave up the valley. He'd polished his club and everything. He reckoned one sharp smack over the head and she'd be his.[4] Hurling his lunch at a low-flying Pteranodon, he thought to himself: "There must be more to life than this!"

The Pteranodon, for her part, thought: "Why's he doing that? I'm a vegetarian!"

1. In the interests of sexual equality, I'm quite happy if you want to call him Carol.
2. And as anyone with even a modest knowledge of primitive history will tell you, Acanthopolis grease is pretty well impossible to get out, even after soaking overnight in Radion.
3. Well, actually he probably spoke, but it was quite difficult to tell the difference in those days.
4. They knew a thing or two about wooing in those days!

16

But in that single moment, Lionel learned one of the great truths of civilization: *knowledge is power*. Well, he didn't actually realize it right at that very moment. It took years of disappointment and failure. But this book isn't just about Lionel, so let's condense the process.

So, what knowledge did Lionel have that set him apart from other primates and made him powerful? Well, for instance, he realized that if you stuck your hand into a fire, it caused your arm to jerk sharply and your mouth to go "Ouch!"[1] What's more, it hurt. There were other things he knew as well, of course, such as the best wood to make pointy sticks out of, and how to stop Diplodocus hide chafing you and causing a nasty rash on your inside leg.[2] This was useful knowledge, and as such it was probably the sort of thing that was worth passing on to other primitives – the sort of thing they might even *pay* for, even though money hadn't been invented yet. And thus the first fee-paying school was born, where – for a couple of pounds of Stegosaurus meat, or a Davy Crockett hat made out of Euoplocephalus hide – you could learn all about pointy stick-making or basic chafe-free tailoring.

Naturally, as primitive man became more sophisticated,[3] education had to develop to keep up. Communication became important and writing was invented. Up until then, it had all been berry-juice drawings. I mean, if you wanted to send a letter to your mum who lived three valleys away across the swamp, you had to draw your message on the side of a rock the size of a house. The schools stepped in and taught an alphabet. OK, so in

1. Or "Ugg!" probably in Lionel's case, but it meant roughly the same thing.
2. This was very useful, since there were no doctors to speak of. There weren't even any doctors to keep completely quiet about, either.
3. Sophisticated may be too strong a word. Less mind-numbingly stupid is probably a better description.

those days it was fairly basic,[1] but at least it was a start. This first school was probably called the Dunroamin Academy for Inquisitive Cavedwellers.[2] And, because it was fee-paying, it supported the other great truth: *learning is for the rich!*

1. Actually it consisted of: Agg, Bugg, Cogg, Digg, Egg, Fugg, Gugg, Hegg, Igg, Jogg, Kugg, Lugg, Mugg, Nog, Ogg, Pogg, Qugg, Rugg, Scagg, Tigg, Ugg (the most important letter in the ancient alphabet), Vugg, Wugg, Xugg, Yugg, Zigg.
2. Later, with the introduction of more comprehensive education policies, it would be called Dunroamin Polytechnic and later still The University of Dunroamin.

TEACHING IN A TOGA

Yes! Even the enlightened early civilizations believed that learning should be restricted to the upper classes – that is to say: the rulers of the land, their families, relatives, friends, dogs, and so forth, plus anyone who could afford to pay.

There were a number of very good reasons for this:[1]

1 The old adage that "knowledge is power" still held true. The feeling was that if you educated the ordinary folk (or *plebs* as the Romans called them), they'd start asking tricky questions such as: "Why is Caesar living in a big posh house, and I'm living in a pile of dung with a dent in the front?" No. It was much better to keep them stupid. After all, "ignorance is bliss", apparently.
2 If poor people were given schooling, they'd have to be given homework, and they didn't really have homes to do their homework in (see point **1**).
3 The schools were private, and the people who owned them didn't really want poor people wandering about the place, leaving little trails of dung and poking at the antiques.

This brings us to the nature of schools. The early schools were often founded by philosophers – people who did a lot of thinking. They thought things like, "I want a big house and a Golf GTi Chariot," and, what is

---

1. You'll notice that I'm using a very unusual interpretation of the term "very good reasons". This interpretation means that they were actually very bad reasons, but everyone managed to persuade themselves that they were very good reasons.

more, they got these things, mainly because they were very bright. But in order to justify having all these goodies, they started schools so that they could teach rich young men how to get themselves elected to the Senate, how to get big houses, etc. Often these schools were housed in the magnificent gardens belonging to the philosophers' homes, which is another good reason why no poor people founded schools in this period. They didn't have gardens. They didn't even have window boxes. Well, certainly not ones large enough to hold a row of wealthy young men learning the 3 Rs, anyway!

The Romans, being educated, realized that the world was full of riches just waiting to be taken. OK, so these riches already belonged to somebody else, but that somebody else was uneducated, so how could they possibly appreciate them? No, it made far more sense to relieve them of this tiresome wealth.

Thus the Romans set out to conquer the world and get rich quick. Of course, they wouldn't make the mistake of educating any of the people they conquered. "Knowledge is power," remember, and that's the last thing you give someone if you want them to appreciate you stealing all their property. In fact, this is the first rule of conquering.[1]

HEY THOSE ROMAN'S ARE CARTING OFF OUR CULTURAL TREASURES!

WHAT IS CULTURAL TREASURES?

You have to take your hat off to the Romans – they were very good at it.[2] But, like all people who are very good at things, they suffered from the sin of pride (although of course they didn't realize it was a sin, because the Ten Commandments hadn't really caught on in any big way at this point). But nevertheless, as we all

1. Not to be confused with the first rule of conkers, which is "Make sure you've got a decent bit of string."
2. In fact, if you didn't take your hat off to the ancient Romans, you were likely to get your head nailed to the floor. They were pretty hot on protocol. Well, they were educated, weren't they?

know, pride comes before a fall, and the Roman Empire had its very own spectacular fall. So spectacular, in fact, that they named it after themselves – they called it the Fall of the Roman Empire.[1]

First the Romans had to visit Britain. Now, your average Ancient Briton was about as barbaric as you could get,[2] but they had failed totally to resist any attempt to invade them. On the other hand, they managed to resist any attempt to educate them.[3]

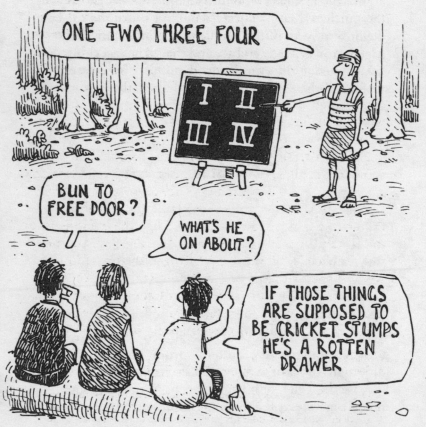

1. Not to be confused with the Fall of the Hackney Empire, which was brought about by too many variety shows containing tripe jugglers.
2. Bit like your modern Brits, really!
3. Also a bit like your modern Brit.

BRITAIN BEFORE THE FALL
(AND IN THE SUMMER)

On the face of it, Caesar's trip to Britain wasn't going to be any different from his invasion of France, except that he wouldn't be expected to eat frogs. In fact, unlike the French, who fought back and swore a lot (not that it had any effect, because none of the Romans spoke French), the Ancient Brits were a pushover. Once they'd been conquered, which took about twenty minutes, they were perfectly happy to stand around all day, covered in woad,[1] and watch the Romans build roads, aqueducts, viaducts, and every other type of duct. They also built cities, baths, and hundreds of villas – huge villas.[2] All of which left the Britons nonplussed,[3] which in turn irritated the Romans.

Caesar started to think that this complacency was some sort of plot,[4] and that one day they would rise up against him. He decided to get friendly with the chief Britons. Invite them to parties, play Twister with them – that sort of thing. However, it soon became obvious that the Brits were not natural party animals. For one thing they smelled (well, they only changed their woad once a week).[5] They also had no small-talk, which as you know is essential at parties (at least until someone turns the lights out). Though to be fair to the Ancient Brits, they did have two topics of conversation: woad, and which

1. Blue paint, B&Q, 4p for five litres.
2. Some of these villas were massive. The one in Aston, Birmingham, was so vast that it now houses a football team.
3. Oh, yes, Queen Boadicea did attempt to fight back, but the Romans just thought that this was typical of a woman, and didn't really take her seriously.
4. He didn't understand the Brits at all. The only thing complicated about them was their language. It still is!
5. On a Wednesday, which was then called Woad-on-s-day.

bit of any animal you couldn't eat.[1] This, plus the fact that the local wine wasn't up to much,[2] persuaded the Romans to break the Golden Rule of Conquering, and educate the Brits.

The rest is history. Caesar was recalled to Rome and stabbed in the back, and the Brits went back to standing around doing nothing. And, despite numerous attempts by other nations to change this, the Brits have to date totally failed to get even a basic grip of the 3 Rs. Or, should I say, the 4 Rs, because it was around this time that much of the known world became Christian.

1. Which is basically any bit below the waist, not counting the legs.
2. A strange mixture of woodcock droppings and tree-bark, with a secret ingredient – which I can now reveal was human sweat.

TOOLS OF THE TRADE

In order to spread the Christian message, it became essential to conquer other countries. With the spread of Christianity came a great need to educate people on a much larger scale. The logic was simple: if you wanted people to read the bible, it wasn't a lot of use if they couldn't read. Of course, there were those who believed that not being able to read was no excuse for not reading the Bible, notably the Spanish Inquisition. They used violence, aggression and even torture to make sure that everyone was correctly educated – a tradition that still survives to this day.[1]

1. In some schools!

And, of course, if you were going to teach people to read, why not teach them to add up at the same time? Not that addition particularly helps with Bible study, but it can't do any harm, can it?[1]

Thus it was that the Church took responsibility for much of the world's education. After all, they had some of the best buildings and, as we have already seen, you can't have a good school without a good building.[2] Because the Church was providing most of the schools, most of the earliest teachers were monks. They made

HE'S TAKEN A VOW OF SILENCE

very good teachers, although most of what they taught was in Latin. Not that this mattered that much because all of the Bible was in Latin, so it made it easier to read if you knew the language. Whether a good knowledge of Latin helped with maths is another story.

1. This shows a basic misunderstanding of the power of mathematics.
2. True though this is, thinking seems to have been reversed over the years, and these days it seems to be essential for a school building to be falling down.

ALL TIGHTS AND TUTORING

The middle of the fifteenth century marks the start of a period known as the Renaissance.[1] It was a great period of learning and exploration. Shakespeare wrote his plays during this period,[2] and Columbus discovered America[3] (almost).[4] Trade between cultures became a reality.

Merchants, often lowly born, became very powerful men. They were known as "the cream of society". This was because they were rich and thick. But, because they *were* so rich, they were able to buy themselves an education. They hired home-tutors.[5] Some even built schools, which they named after themselves or their business.

Others simply contributed to existing schools, in exchange for a place on the school's Board of Governors. This gave them control over how things were taught at that school, even though they knew diddly squat about teaching and often couldn't hold a pencil, let alone write their own name. But they knew the truth of the saying "Money talks"![6] Of course, these school buildings were often very basic. After all, there was no point in wasting money. The pupils weren't there to enjoy themselves, they were there to learn. This was a fact that some pupils were apt to forget, and so they had to be given the odd[7] reminder.

1. A French word meaning "rebirth".
2. A good thing.
3. A bad thing.
4. For the full facts about this near-discovery, read my book *The Life and Times of Christobal Colon*.
5. The Open University wasn't on telly in those days, mainly because telly hadn't been invented.
6. If they'd had any education at all, they would have realized that money doesn't have a voice-box, let alone the knowledge of any formalized language.
7. Sometimes very odd. And very frequent too.

SPARE the ROD and SPOIL the CHILD

So said somebody (a teacher, probably). But it was a philosophy that was the watchword of many of these early schools. After all, a bit of physical violence had helped the various heathen nations around the world learn the message of Christianity, and they weren't even paying for it![1] Surely a bit of the same sort of thing could only help the teaching process in schools? Well, whether it did or not, it became the norm. It was nothing for a child to be beaten within an inch of his life, and for his parents to have to pay through the nose for the privilege.[2] Not only that, it was often the case that the more you paid, the better the class of corporal punishment you got. This was mainly because there was a theory in

YES SIR, WE HAVE A SPECIAL INTRODUCTORY OFFER ON BEATINGS WITH A FIRST TERM DISCOUNT FOR THE CANE, AND A CUT RATE PACKAGE OF PUNISHMENT IS THROWN IN IF YOU OPT FOR OUR SIX MONTH-EASY-PAY CREDIT SCHEME

I'M DOOMED

1. Unless you count having to part with their country's natural resources.
2. I would have told my parents I'd rather have the money.

these early schools that you could actually beat knowledge into a child.

Of course, we now realize that this isn't the case. But there was a time when violence in the classroom was the accepted face of education. You only have to read Charles Dickens to realize how true this is.[1] It was still restricted to the wealthy or high-born child, not that the poor kids minded too much. They were far too busy being poked up chimneys on the end of a stick!

1. Don't bother to read it now, there's yards of the stuff! Just take my word for it!

LET'S HAVE A WHIP-ROUND

The school system continued pretty much in this vein for the next few hundred years, using the same buildings with the same facilities, but making the occasional change in teaching methods. For instance, the mid-seventeenth century practice of burning someone at the stake as a witch just because they got all their spellings right[1] was replaced with a public flogging for getting the slightest thing wrong.[2] You must remember that during this time much of the world was at war, and I suppose the various methods of torturing the enemy were first tried out in schools. After all, school is the seat of learning, isn't it?

1. Yes! I do mean right! But then, let's face it, anyone who can get ten out of ten in a spelling test has got to have some kind of magic power! Even teachers can't do that well!
2. Both these teaching practices have now been replaced by sarcasm.

BELT-U-LIKE

Even as recently as the 1950s dingy classrooms were partially lit by the glow of rosy bottoms. There was a range of weapons available[1] for inflicting punishment, but the most usual was the cane – a simple bamboo affair readily available from any decent garden centre. The

WINDOW-BOX CANES   GARDEN CANES   SCHOOL CANES

cane became very popular, because if it got broken by the weekend its owner could easily get a new one and be up and whopping first thing Monday morning.

On the other hand, the headmaster at my own junior school had a thing that was rather inaccurately named "tickling stick". I think this was a reference to the comedian Ken Dodd, who was very popular then and who carried a feather duster also (and more accurately) called a "tickling stick". But the similarity was in name only – the headmaster's was made of leather rather than feathers. Both had a wooden handle, but the headmaster's had three leather thongs and Ken's had none. And the other big difference was that the headmaster didn't say: "Ooh-er, Missus!" as he belted you with it, as Ken is known to do.

What the headmaster did say, rather strangely, was, "This is going to hurt me more than it hurts you."

Really! That's what teachers used to say before they hit you. It makes you wonder how they ever became teachers, doesn't it?

1. Unlike sugar, classroom punishment wasn't rationed in the fifties.

HEAD-MASTER

KEN DODD

Where did they buy such things? I'm referring to the headmaster's tickling stick, not Ken Dodd's duster. I think I'm familiar enough with the ways of the High Street to know that you can get a very fine feather duster at B&Q, but what about a leather bottom-beater? Not that I want one personally, you understand, but I am curious, in the interests of history. Did my old head-master buy it somewhere or did he make it? Do they have weapon-making lessons at teacher training college or is there a special place where teachers can get this stuff? Perhaps they get a discount for being members of the NUT.[1] What sort of a place would sell that kind of thing?

My team and I searched the length and breadth of Britain, leaving no back street unturned, and the only such place we could find was *I. Wackham & Son, Inventors & Manufacturers of Corrective Weaponry to Gentlemen Of The Teaching Profession*. We decided, after much soul-searching (and a large amount of money

1. The National Union of Teachers. Only teachers could belong to a union the initials of whose name spell the word NUT!

33

changing hands), not to print the address here. However, I will tell you that they have a "By Royal Appointment" crest on their wall. As you probably know, a shop can only display the crest if they actually supply the Royal Family with their goods. I thought William and Harry were looking a bit nervous! But if people like I. Wackham sell this stuff, who invents it? Well, we'll probably never know, because that sort of thing is no longer allowed, fortunately.[1]

However, when it was, it wasn't only teachers who meted out corporal punishment. Imagine the situation in, say, a busy minor public school in the mid-fifties. There were so many extra duties for the staff to cope with (coaching the rowing eight, beating the Chess Club,[2] having tea with wealthy parents who were considering donating a new science wing to the school) that there wasn't always a teacher free to attend to a boy who wanted a good hiding. So it often fell to prefects to mete out punishment. And being young men with enquiring minds, their inventiveness was unbounded.[3] Not that

1. Well, fortunately for today's pupils, but not really fortunately for I. Wackham and his family, who were, after all, only trying to make a living.
2. At chess.
3. Unlike some of the victims, who were often bound and gagged.

there were many actual deaths – no more than you'd expect, anyway.

Of course, it wasn't all beatings[1] in these early schools. Oh, no. The pupils had to work as well, because – as we discovered earlier – they weren't there to enjoy themselves. The school curriculum had been expanded by this point to include History,[2] Geography,[3] Physics,[4] Chemistry[5] and Physical Education.[6] And the classrooms had also been expanded to include ordinary kids. Yes! The poor had been dragged kicking and screaming out of the chimneys and into the schools. They were to get an education! They were even allowed to sit next to "a better type of boy", as long as they didn't teach him any nasty habits, of course.

These changes were all due to the 1944 Education Bill. This became an Act of Parliament, named after Bill Somebody, but it basically meant that every child would now get an education. And the really good news was that it was free.[7] Oh! and this bill applied to girls too! Because, as you've probably noticed, there hasn't been much mention of girls up to now. This is because, as I have said elsewhere,[8] it took a very long time for anyone to see any point in educating women. This was probably due to early civilizations' belief in the saying "Knowledge is power". They realized that if women were educated, they'd be able to take over the world!

But we had arrived. From humble beginnings in a distant age, to an age of technology, where education is everything. From a ramshackle, wind-swept hovel with

1. Not quite.
2. Dates.
3. Hills.
4. Electrocuting yourself.
5. Blowing yourself up.
6. More violence.
7. The really *bad* news was that it was compulsory!
8. *Coping with Teachers* – another great title from Hippo Books!

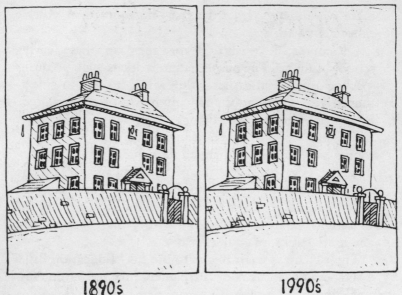

1890's   1990's

no facilities, to a . . . It's amazing how little schools have changed, really! And this is how it has been for the second half of this century. Obviously there have been changes. The syllabus has been expanded and contracted like a demented accordion, educational theories have been tried and abandoned, then tried again. And whatever the changes, the pupils (and teachers) still have to turn up. How do they cope? How do *you* cope? That is what the rest of this book is all about! Read on!

Coping – those first few steps....

No-one, least of all a five-year-old child,[1] could possibly know what lies in store for them as they put on their brand-new[2] school uniform for their very first day at infant school. Yesterday they were happy-go-lucky. Today they're a mixed infant. And they don't know how they feel about that, because they don't really know what it is.

STEP 2.
POUR INTO
MOULD

STEP 3.

FINISHED
INFANT

INSTANT
INFANT
MIX

STEP 1.
MIX IN BOWL

No-one can really prepare you for your first day at school. Of course they can tell you what their first day was like, and I suppose it's possible that yours might be similar, but it's just as likely to be totally different. Can you remember your first day at school? Try. All right, no need to call in the services of a hypnotherapist – it was a rhetorical question.[3] I certainly can't. Oh, I can remember bits. I can remember realizing pretty early on

1. Of course I realize that some children start school younger than five! What do you think I am, stupid or something?
2. Or secondhand. You see, big brothers do have their uses!
3. Which means that I'm not really interested!

that if I volunteered to be Milk Monitor I could get out of almost an entire morning's classes. In fact, when Margaret Thatcher, as Secretary of State for Education, abolished free school milk all those years later, I took it really personally. I reckoned she was only doing it to stop me bunking off lessons, twenty years too late![1] In secondary school I tried the same ploy with notes, but it's really quite hard to persuade teachers that they want to send a note to another teacher, when they clearly have no desire to. In fact, it takes more effort to invent this kind of stuff than it does to pay attention to the lesson in the first place. It only took me five years to realize that! Not bad for a slow learner!

1. She's always had it in for me!

Anyway, cast your mind back. Try to imagine yourself going to school for the very first time. You're neat. You're tidy. You're cleaner than you've ever been, even cleaner than you were that time your mum accidentally put you in the washing machine with a pile of sheets. It wasn't your fault. You would have told her that you were playing Star Trek and the sheets were the *Starship Enterprise*, but you were eighteen months old and could only master basic conversation.[1] Anyway, the important thing was that you survived,[2] and are now standing in the infant school playground, along with all the other new kids.

1. These were usually in your own special code, and involved eating or going to the toilet.
2. Although you now can't watch a Bold commercial without shuddering.

The first thing that strikes you about you and the other kids is this: you all look the same! Yes, identical! Well, uniform will do this every time, as long as you're all wearing it properly.[1] The minute you see this you're gripped with a terrible fear. How about if Mum takes home the wrong kid when she comes to pick you up? Oh, no! It could be *weeks* before she realizes her mistake! Especially if she takes home Darren Formby 'cos he's so wet he'll never speak up for himself, will he? He could be living in your house, sleeping in your bed, and sucking your teddy's ear for *ever*! And you might have to go and live with gypsies![2] You panic. Your stomach starts to churn, turn over, and trickle down your leg. You think about running,[3] but are stopped by the bell.[4] The older kids start to file into the school. They are six and have been going to school for *ages*, so they really know the ropes.[5] The other new kids seem to be following them, but you hesitate.

"It's all right," says a friendly voice at your shoulder. "We're all going into the hall."

Who *is* this woman? Do you know her? You've never seen her before, and even though she looks very friendly, she could be wearing a latex mask. You've been told never to talk to strange people, and nothing

1. Skirts and trousers on the bottom half, shirts and blouses on top.
2. It was a very common fear when I was child to think you might find yourself living in a gypsy camp. It's only now that I've grown up that I realize that, although it would probably be fun, they wouldn't actually *want* me!
3. Which isn't that easy with damp legs.
4. – or whistle or cattle prod, or whatever else schools use to get pupils' attention.
5. In Victorian times, they would probably have been dangled from the ropes quite regularly.

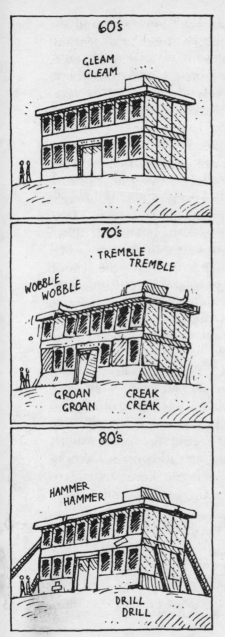

60's

GLEAM
GLEAM

70's

TREMBLE
TREMBLE

WOBBLE
WOBBLE

GROAN
GROAN

CREAK
CREAK

80's

HAMMER
HAMMER

DRILL
DRILL

could be stranger than a woman who hangs around school playgrounds in a latex mask pretending to be nice, could it? But maybe she's harmless. Mad, but harmless. Ah, yes! But thousands of Russians thought they'd won a skiing holiday when they got on the train to the salt mines of Siberia. Mind you, they didn't have the benefit of an English State Education, did they? Anyway, here you are, a five-year-old mixed infant, following a friendly-looking woman (who may or may not be wearing a latex mask) into the main hall on your very first day in school.

Let's have a look at this school as we hurry to catch up with the others. It's one of those square affairs that look as if they're built entirely out of glass and pre-stressed Ryvita. They were built in the sixties, fell apart in the seventies, but were still being used in the eighties. In fact, they're still being used in the nineties, but they're now in such a bad state that even the vandals don't bother with them. They were designed in such a way that the hall was the centre-point of the school, with all the classrooms arranged around it. This had certain advantages. For instance, if someone fell off the wall bars in a gym class, the entire school could be in there pointing and laughing within seconds.

And that's where you are now. In the hall. But you're not laughing.[1] Far from it. You're much too nervous. There's an overpowering smell of soap, which is odd because schools usually smell of badly-cooked food (*see also* **Meals, school**), not soap. Don't worry, it won't last. Most of these kids have only washed because it's their first day and they want to make a good impression. They won't wash again until they day they start work, if they ever do. However, the smell of soap is comforting. You start to relax. Maybe relax is an overstatement, but you loosen up your neck muscles enough to allow your head to turn about six degrees in either direction. This gives you a slightly better view of the hall.

It's quite a homely sort of place, really – quite friendly. That red stain on the wall probably isn't actually blood. Just because it's in the shape of a body, that doesn't have to mean it was made by someone facing a firing squad, does it?[2] And as for the woman doing all the talking, who you later discover is the head

1. But then no-one's fallen off the wall bars. Not yet, anyway.
2. You later discover the true story behind the red stain. Some years previously it was decided to decorate the hall for Christmas and the various classes were invited to submit items for inclusion. Gemma Stensil (class 3) painted a huge Father Christmas. It took the entire school's yearly supply of red paint, but it won her a good badge – a good badge that she immediately lost again when it was discovered that the paint had seeped through the cheap old kitchen paper and on to the wall. The fact that this was due to Ms Taggly hanging the picture before it was dry was deemed irrelevant, because teachers are never wrong and are not allowed to take the blame for anything.

teacher – just because she's eighteen metres tall with warts and a moustache, that doesn't mean she's a nasty person, does it? She probably isn't actually shouting, just talking loudly enough for everyone to hear. Even though it's damaging your inner ear, it doesn't mean she's doing it on purpose, does it? Of course it doesn't, you reassure yourself. In fact, you're getting to quite like the hall. In fact, you're getting to *really* like it. In fact, you're getting to feel that spending the day in here wouldn't be so bad after all. And just as you and the hall are starting to become good pals, you're on the move again. Wouldn't you know it? But then, that's Murphy's Law.

So where are we off to this time? you wonder as you gather up your many belongings: gym-kit bag, Thomas the Tank Engine lunchbox with fitted flask, small paper bag with an apple in it for break-time, spare tissues, first aid kit, etc., etc. You haven't even had time to take your coat off. You're working up quite a sweat. The poor kid next to you must be really boiling – he's standing in a pool of perspiration. I suppose it *is* perspiration. You'll never know, because you're being swept up in a sea of eager, enquiring

43

minds, atop sweating, flailing bodies, all heading for a door that you can see they're never going to get through[1]. Where are we going? To a *classroom*, whatever that is!

1. And this is *before* you've had any education!

Top of the class : a new and moving experience..

Once the confusion dies down and you're safely in your classroom, you get a chance to breathe. You also realize that not all of the 400-odd[1] kids who were in the hall are going to be stuffed into this classroom, which is a good thing, because it's way too small to get them all in, even if they were stacked in layers, one on top of the other.[2]

"Cor!" you think to yourself. "If they'd all come in here it would have been just like the Black Hole of Calcutta!"[3]

So this is a classroom, then, is it? This is going to be your home for the next year, is it? That woman in the BHS cardigan is going to be your teacher, is she? What *is* a teacher, anyway? you wonder to yourself. You'll find out soon enough! But first you have to sort out some important things, such as:

1) Hands up all those having school dinners. The teacher already knows the answer to this one, because your mum and dad had to fill in a form. She's just checking whether you know or not. You'll soon discover that teachers do a lot of this sort of thing – checking to see if you know something. They call it teaching, you call it invasion of privacy.[4] However, it may surprise you to

---

1. Some very odd.
2. Oh, no! I shouldn't have written that! If some education bigwig is reading, I've probably given them ideas!
3. Except of course you wouldn't think that because you're only five and you haven't even *heard* of the Black Hole of Calcutta.
4. At least you would if you had the foggiest idea what it meant!

know that there are quite a lot of children who don't know the answer to this question and are totally mystified as to why they're carrying a lunchbox to school every day. But then, they're only five, which should explain their confusion. (However, it doesn't explain why they're still confused about it when they leave school at sixteen.)

2) Which peg are you going to hang your coat on? You've got your eye on the one with the Thunderbirds label, but because Dean Wavy pushes in, you get lumbered with Polly Pockets instead. Oh, well, you can draw a beard on her when nobody's looking and that'll make her look like a mad mutant. Great!

3) Name-tags. Some schools insist that everything is labelled with the child's name. Everything, that is, except the child.[1] Teachers are very thorough about labels. After all, they've got enough to think about just stuffing heads full of facts, without having to worry about whether everyone's wearing the right socks or not. It's best to get this sorted out at the outset, so the labels have to be checked. Of course methods of doing this vary from area to area. We heard of one school where the new kids have to strip off and throw all their clothes[2] into a pile in the middle of the room, then try to find their own stuff. This sorts out who can read as well as who's labelled their clobber. Not surprisingly, it

NOT THAT FAR SIMON

usually turns out that most of the kids are correctly labelled, but none of them know it. But after all, that's one of the reasons you go to school in the first place – to learn how to spell your own name.[3]

1. Although my research team did discover one school that liked the children to be labelled.
2. And I do mean *all*.
3. One teacher we heard of wouldn't let the children in her care put their clothes on again until they could read their labels. This so restricted the career opportunities of one poor lad, that when he left school the only job he could get was caretaker at a nudist camp.

4) The toilets. As every teacher knows, it's very important to make sure that all the new kids know where the toilets are, for pretty obvious reasons. This is probably much more important than most people realize. You see, according to experts,[1] what you learn in your first five years can make or break you in later life. So obviously if you haven't cracked the lav by the time you're five you've got no chance, have you?

5) Spare clothing. Most infant schools insist that children bring a change of clothing in a bag, again for obvious reasons! After all, little children have accidents even before they start school. So given that they are now in the same building as a few hundred other kids, their chances of meeting with an accident are increased several-fold. This accident could be anything from wetting themselves to something fatal – particularly if there's a caretaker around.[2]

One of my researchers, Lauden Forthright, assures me that when he was a headmaster, his school insisted that every pupil provide the following:

1) Spare school uniform
2) A suit
3) Full evening dress for formal occasions (i.e. school dances)
4) Frogman's suit (the school was very damp)
5) Gas mask (he had a secret fear that the Germans might invade, even though the war had been over for years).

I didn't understand the need for a suit. He explained that every time a parent came to the school to complain, the caretaker would warn him of their approach from his

1. Spock believes this. So do Scottie, Kirk and Bones.
2. For this reason some schools insist on children being insured.

48

ESSENTIAL ITEMS OF SCHOOL CLOTHING

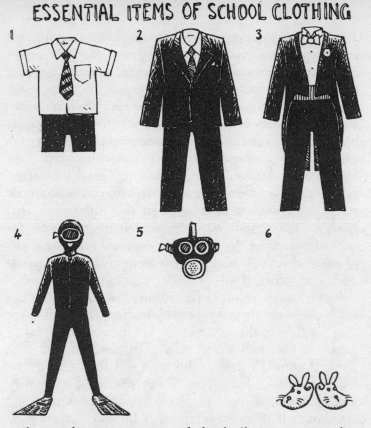

tank-proof turret on top of the boiler room. Lauden would then get the entire school to change into suits and persuade the angry parent that this was not in fact a school, but an office building full of dwarves. It worked every time, but since parents were always arriving to complain, the children got very little work done. I tactfully pointed out to him that this could only have caused more parents to complain, thus making the situation worse. He should have taken the advice of one headteacher I heard of, who simply put a sign outside the school reading DANGER – CARETAKER ON PREMISES. That did the trick!

Anyway, having got your name tags, extra clothing and peg sorted out, and having found out that you aren't eating school dinners after all,[1] you're now ready to be educated. It's quite possible that you went to play-school, so you'll be familiar with the idea of sitting down among a group of children of your own age, eating playdough and sticking bits of coloured paper onto each others' heads to the amusement of a couple of nice cosy ladies called Auntie This and Auntie That,[2] then stopping for a glass of milk, a story and maybe even a little sleep. You were probably given the impression that going to playschool was supposed to prepare you for real school. Even the name, Playschool, suggests a sort of pretend school. Well, if you were given this impression, you were lied to!

Playschool is about as far from real school as you can get.[3] Oh, yes, Primary School teachers are still quite cosy, still have the same sweet smiles and thick cardigans, but they're not beyond yelling at you if you cross them. Auntie This never did that, did she? And if you fell over, she cuddled you, didn't she? Not here, they won't! If you fall over, you have to pick yourself up and take yourself off to the secretary, who will measure your cut, then check in the rule book to find out if it's long enough to warrant a plaster. This will probably then go on your school record:

1. Yes! That stuff your mum gave you in the plastic box with Thomas The Tank Engine on the side is *food*. Make the most of it. It's all you're getting all day!
2. Of course they aren't really called Auntie This and Auntie That. I've changed their names to protect the innocent. Also to protect my daughter, who still goes to playschool.
3. Actually you *can* get further away from real school, but this involves running away to sea.

This child keeps falling over. She's costing us a fortune in plasters. Do you think her parents could be persuaded to move to another town?

Oh, yes! This is a very different place! However, you are still a far cry from what most of us remember as school. This is just a taster.

So you settle in. It's not so bad. You're making new friends, you can find your way around, and you've learned to recognize the signs when Mrs Jumbly is about to explode. At seven you're a real old hand. You find yourself showing some of the new kids the ropes.[1] You actually find yourself enjoying school. You even – I can hardly believe it – start playing the recorder! How could you? There's really no hope for you now! Don't get too cosy, though – you're about to be moved on! But first they're going to give you a long summer holiday. You don't realize this at the time, but they're doing this to soften the blow!

1. And occasionally tying them up with them.

Piggy in the middle school

Your first day at infant school now seems a million years ago. But here you are again, standing in a strange playground, waiting to find out what they're going to do to you. A couple of months ago you were one of the old kids, now you're one of the new kids again. Have you shrunk, or has everybody else got bigger?

You look around for familiar faces. All your class from the infant school were coming to the junior school with you, weren't they? A terrible thought strikes you! What if they all met with freak accidents over the summer holidays? After all, you went away to your Auntie Beryl's in Scotland for the summer, didn't you?[1] You haven't seen any of them since you got back, have you? Anything could have happened to them! They could all have left town,[2] been swept away by gales, who knows what!

Ah! Hang on! Just as your mind races away, your brain catches up with it. You've spotted Teresa Cork. Phew! She was in your class. At last – a friendly face, buried somewhere under those spots (probably). OK, so you never liked her; OK, so she stinks; but at least her presence disproves the freak accident/gales theories. You wave. Just a little wave. One that says, "Hi, Teresa!" but definitely doesn't say, "Come over here!"

What? She's ignoring you? She saw you but she's too busy playing with her . . . big sister! Big sister! She must be desperate! But that's it, isn't it? All the others have

---

1. Which was awful! You'd rather have been fed to the caretaker's dog! At least he would have appreciated you.
2. Driven away by irate school secretaries who've gone over-budget on their sticking plaster allowance.

got big sisters! Or . . . what's the other thing, with trousers and a runny nose? That's it! Big brothers! Yeah! And you haven't. You told your mum it would give you problems in later life, not having a big brother, but would she listen? Does she ever!

So here you are, alone again in an alien environment – junior school. However, once you get over the initial shock, you find that it's not unlike Infant School. Oh, yes, you don't have "choosing time" any more and there's less Lego lying around, but it's not really that bad. You've progressed from recorder to triangle.[1] You

1. Well, *I* call that a progression!

might even get to play in the school concert, and you're hotly tipped for a major rôle in the school play. People are still talking about your wise man in the Infant School Nativity play. Not so much for the regal qualities you brought to the rôle, but more for the fact that you got a bit bored during the singing of the full version of *We Wish You a Merry Christmas*,[1] started swinging your jam-jar full of myrrh around and knocked poor Mary out. Serves her right! She was putting you off during your best bit by humming Madonna's *Like a Virgin* under her breath. (*See also* **Play, school**.)

1. What *is* figgy pudding, anyway?

Yes, you're settling in nicely. You've even survived the National Curriculum testing. Not that many of the staff have – they've cracked under the strain of all the extra paperwork. Well, teachers aren't used to filling in forms, are they? Most of them can only write their names in chalk, and even then it's not joined up. But twenty-seven nervous breakdowns in one term? That's got to be something of a record. You start to feel almost sorry for them, which is worrying because your natural instinct is to distrust teachers and revel in their discomfort. But after you've been allowed to bring your Gamegear to school for the third day running because there's nobody left in the county who's qualified to teach you, you're soon back to normal. Actually, they did bring the school crossing lady in one day to take a class, they were so desperate, but it soon became clear that she knew less than you lot did. In fact, she didn't even have a basic grasp of the *Highway Code*, which probably explains why she gets knocked down so much.[1]

And so you continue to settle in, the school growing around you like an old coat.[2] You know which teachers can be persuaded to send you on an errand and which ones it's best to avoid; which ones think you're cute, and which ones know you're not. You've even survived the new experience of being taught by men, because it wasn't something you encountered at infant school. Male teachers are far less common there. You certainly never spotted any, anyway. There were a couple of women teachers you thought might be dressed up and hiding from the police, but there was nobody you called Sir.

1. Although it's far more likely that the real reason for this is that she's married to the caretaker, and most of the drivers in the area are ex-pupils!
2. In fact it's exactly like an old coat – it's far too small and it lets in the rain.

Anyway, all in all, taken by and large, this junior school is OK. You could get to like it. In fact . . . you're starting to get a warm feeling you've experienced before. But when? Not when you were a baby, because the warm feeling then meant that you'd wet the bed, but more recently. That's it! When you were seven! That's when you last felt this cosy I-could-stay-here-for-ever feeling. When you were seven. Your last term at infant school. Your last term, just before . . . oh, dear! You remember what happened next, don't you? That's right! You went on a long summer holiday, after which . . . you changed schools!

Big school, big problems

They're like rare birds feeding on a marsh – nervously neat, timidly talking like small birds pecking. A cry goes up from somewhere. They scatter, alarmed by a gun. The place becomes a ghost town. The only sound is a creak as the battered old boiler-room door swings on its hinges, until slammed shut by the battered old caretaker. Who are these shadowy figures appearing on the horizon, silhouetted against a cloud-filled sky like the Four Horsemen of the Apocalypse, even if there are only two

four horsemen of the Apocalypse

Death   Pestilence   Darren   Wayne

of them? Don't you know? They're BIG KIDS. You've heard about them. They're the stuff of legend and nightmare. They eat first-years, you've heard,[1] but not before they've made you cry and mess your pants, then stuffed your head down the toilet. Now logic should tell you that after all that, you'd be pretty well inedible to anyone other than some poor soul on the point of starvation, but it doesn't. You're still terrified. And I must admit that if you're eleven, there's something far more terrifying about a fifteen-year-old than if you're seven and being confronted by a ten-year-old. This probably has something to do with the fact that everyone seems to do a huge amount of growing between the ages of eleven and fifteen.[2] As you cower in terror, you find time to ask yourself, "Why are they after *me*?"

They aren't particularly. They're after any first-year.

"But why? What on earth have I ever done to them?"

"I mean, I don't even know them, do I?"

The answers to these questions, in the order you asked them, are:

1. You're heard it from someone who heard it from someone who . . . etc., etc., but that doesn't stop you believing it. Boy, do you need educating or what!
2. Except me!

Question 1: They don't know. But when *they* were first-years, the fifth-formers came after *them*. It's tradition, and they've been looking forward to it all year. Please don't spoil their fun!

Question 2: Nothing, I imagine. After all, they're a lot bigger than you are.

Question 3: How should I know? After all, I don't even know *you*, do I, let alone any of your friends?

What is about to happen to you is called an initiation ceremony. They are part of our heritage, and have helped make Britain great (probably). It's quite likely that something of the sort was practised by the British army as they conquered the rest of the world,[1] before they were told to give it back.[2]

1. According to the history books.
2. According to fact.

However, whatever the deep-seated psychological reasons behind initiation ceremonies, they can be handled. To find out how to do this, refer to the A–Z section of this book, which is further along.

Recently, I found these extracts from my own school diaries. They may have some bearing on the subject. I was clearing out some old furniture from the loft, when I came across some dusty old drawers. Not being one to waste things, I tried them on. They didn't look bad. Anyway, in among the other stuff I found my diaries, and after a quick dust and a cough, I turned to my first day at school, and found this:

Firs day at BIG Skool. Oh, no!!!!!!!!!!!!!! I was up all nite been sik. I desided too tak all my munny out of the bank,[1] an use it to bribe the Big Kids. That'l werk![2] Got too skool. Sore Micky Shorthouse. He wos criing – big baby!!!! Colin Butler, who iz clever an iz my new best friend[3] had gott a role of wallpapper with briks on it. He said that iff we rapped ourselfz up in it, the Bigg Bois wood think wee were a wall, an ignore uss, an knot stuf uz down the toolet Latter, when we wuz dryin our hairs, we told him hee wus stoopid, an not to bother talkin too uz ever ever agen !!!!! ! !!???!!!!!!!????!!![4]

1. It was a plastic pig, actually.
2. It didn't.
3. Best friend, that is, apart from virtually everyone else in the school including the caretaker.
4. As you can see, I was pretty good at spelling even then!

What this shows, I think, is that even *I* had to go through this initiation, yet I survived intact. The nightmares have pretty well stopped, I don't have therapy any more, and I'm reliably informed that I will eventually be able to use a proper lavatory without having to get someone to stand on guard outside.

So this is Big School. Of course it's not all initiation ceremonies. You get detention, lines and other punishments as well. And lessons. But what exactly is this Big School like? Has your time at primary school prepared you for it? Well, yes and no. Obviously some things are the same. You'll still be expected to do writing, reading sums, and stuff like that. You won't necessarily be expected to continue learning the recorder, unless of course the therapy hasn't worked and you need to. You probably won't be expected to continue with that other great feature of junior school . . . country dancing! Yes! I'd almost forgotten that! Country dancing! Aaagh! If you ever need proof that teachers have ways of getting their own back by humiliating you in public, just watch a country dancing demonstration! I know! I belonged to my junior school's country dancing team! To get the full gruesome truth about country dancing, refer to the A–Z section of this book.

School: the big adventure

But let's now concern ourselves with Big School, and just what you have let yourself in for. Try this simple decision-making exercise.

Read from number 1, make your decision, then follow the instructions. It's that simple!

1 It's your first day at secondary school. You are nervously hovering at the gate. Do you:
a Go in? If so, go to **18**.
b Run away? If so, go to **15**.
c Linger longer? Go to **16**.

2 This impresses them. They let you off. Do you:
a Say: "Can I join your gang?" Go to **6**.
b Say: "Don't try that again, OK?" Go to **20**.
c Ask them if they remember *The Woodentops*? Go to **16**.

3 You find yourself in a beautiful garden. School seems worlds away. Do you:
a Stay there? Go to **15**.
b Get out quick! Go to **11**.
c Start picking the flowers for your secret love? Go to **21**.

4 They accept your bribe, and let you go. Very pleased with yourself, you run away around the side of the school. Do you:

a Think you know where you're going? Go to **15**.

b Don't care, but just run? Go to **3**.

c Stop and think, "I wonder where this goes?" Go to **21**.

5 You impress the teachers, but alienate everyone else. Do you:

a Try to wriggle out of the situation? Go to **11**.

b Don't care and let them be annoyed? Go to **16**.

c Shrug feebly? Go to **16**.

6 They laugh in your face, and tell you to get lost! Do you:

a Run away and try to find a hole to crawl into? Go to **3**.

b Say, "suit yourself!" and walk away? Go to **20**.

c Ask them what they think they're laughing at? Go to **21**.

7 This only makes it worse. They hand you over to the Ninja Monitors. Do you:

a Try to bribe them? Go to **4**.

b Go quietly? Go to **10**.

c Say, "You're not real Ninjas!" Go to **16**.

8 Your best mate is now going out with this person you really fancy. Do you:

a Say, "Oh, well, never mind!" Go to **13**.

b Decide to let this person know how you feel? Go to **20**.

c Fight him/her for her/him? Go to **16**.

9 You're at the cinema during school hours with your new friend, and you spot some older kids from your school sitting nearby. Do you:

a Hide? Go to **11**.

b Wave? Go to **13**.

c Report the older kids to a teacher? Go to **5**.

d Carry on snogging? **21**.

10 You find yourself in your new classroom. Do you:

a Sit near the front, looking keen? Go to **14**.

b Hide away at the back? Go to **7**.

c Ask to be excused immediately? Go to **15**.

11 Ooops! Wrong! The bullies get to hear about it, and give you grief! Do you:

a Try to buy them off? Go to **4**.

b Tell them to get lost? Go to **20**.

c Say, "Can we talk about this?" Go to **21**.

12 The fifth-years catch you and try to stick your head down the toilet. Do you:

a Struggle? Go to **7**.

b Let them get on with it? Go to **2**.

c Offer to help? Go to **16**.

13 You get away with it. Do you:

a Now believe yourself to be invincible? Go to **7**.

b Put it down to luck, and don't try anything like it again? Go to **20**.

c Try it again? Go to **16**.

14 Nobody likes a swot. Some other kids threaten to get you at playtime. Do you:
a Tell your big brother/sister? Go to **7**.
b Say, "Fine! See you, then!" Go to **2**.
c Offer to do all their homework? Go to **21**.

15 You get eaten by the caretaker's dog. Sorry!

16 Wrong! Go to **15**.

17 You are going out with the most stunning person in the school, and it's still only your first day! Do you:
a Tell everyone about your good fortune? Go to **11**.
b Decide to keep your relationship a secret? Go to **9**.
c Tell your best mate? Go to **21**.

18 You see an old friend from junior school. They seem to know the ropes. They warn you about initiation ceremonies, and advise you that the only thing to do is hide. Do you:
a Hide? Go to **12**.
b Stand around waiting for the fifth-years to grab you? Go to **3**.
c Ignore them? Go to **16**.

19 You find a secret tunnel. Do you:
   a Go down it? Go to **3**.
   b Report it? Go to **5**.
   c Ignore it? Go to **16**.

20 This really impresses this stunning girl/boy that you always fancied in junior school, but never had the courage to ask out. Do you:
   a Seize your chance and ask them out? Go to **17**.
   b Get your best mate to ask them for you? Go to **8**.
   c Find another way of letting them know? Go to **6**.
   d Get pathetic about it? Go to **16**.

21 Error of judgement! Go to **15**.

GO
BACK

As you will see from the above exercise, whatever you do, you're likely to get eaten by the caretaker's dog, which is symbolic of any terrible fate. Incidentally, if you found that you didn't get eaten, but kept going round and round in circles getting nowhere, this just goes to show what school life is all about: going around in ever decreasing circles, getting nowhere, until you eventually fall down the plughole, out through the waste-pipe and on to the scrap-heap.

ADVERTISEMENT

DON'T GET SCRAPPED, GET "COPING WITH SCHOOL"©

Of course you can be taught how to cope with the whole sorry business, and that's where the next section of this book should help. Because the world of school is so complex and mysterious, I've provided you with an A–Z of as much useful knowledge, hints and observations as I can cram into this small volume. Obviously I've missed some things out. For example, I've steered clear of teachers,[1] partly because I've dealt with them in greater detail elsewhere,[2] and partly because they're fellow travellers on this great journey, even if they're facing in a different direction from everyone else! But don't pass my advice on to them. If they haven't discovered how to cope by now, they never will!

Ground plan of a typical school...

Overleaf is the ground plan of a typical school. The name plate has been removed to protect the inmates. Actually it was removed by a DIY enthusiast and converted into three shelves and a cat-flap. Most of the windows have been removed by vandals, and the roof came off during the Under Thirteen Less Homework riots of 1987. The school was painted by the PTA at weekends. Oh yes, like most schools, this one has had a chequered past. For a while it also had a chequered floor, when some of the PTA volunteers decided to get creative with the paintbrush.

So you see, all in all just a typical school. Even though this school may not be in your area, I feel sure there's one exactly like it. In fact you may even go to it! Turn the page to find out . . .

1. Always good advice!
2. *Coping With Teachers*. Get it now!

School plan...

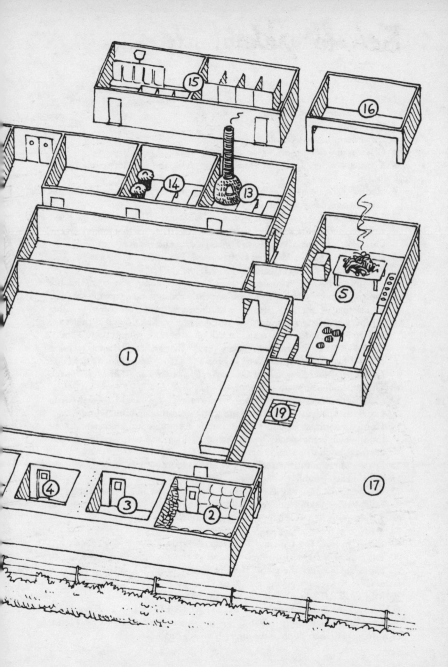

Key for school plan...

1 Hall – used for assemblies, concerts, torture by recorder, force-feeding by school dinners, and death by caretaker's dog.
2 Classroom – padded.
3 Classroom – sound-proof.
4 Classroom – riot-proof.
5 Kitchen – where food can enter as real meat and veg and come out as mush.
6 Medical Room – where pupils can enter as perfectly healthy students, and come out as jibbering hypochondriacs.
7 School Library – or at least it would be but somebody borrowed the book and forgot to return it (they also forgot to read it, it was that interesting!).
8 Caretaker's *En Suite* Bathroom/Toilet/Jacuzzi and Bidet.
9 Caretaker's *En Suite* Morning Coffee Break Lounge.
10 Broom Cupboard – permanently locked.
11 Theatre – where the school play takes place. This room is so small that the audience can only sit in pairs. Consequently the audience viewing rota and the casting of the play are done at the same time. Wherever possible brothers and sisters etc. are cast in the same scenes. Identical twins are always welcomed at this particular school, where they tend to do a lot of those "very funny mistaken identity plays" that Shakespeare was so good at (ones like *Two Gentlemen of Verona* and *Two Blokes Who Really Look Like Each Other Except That One is Really Wealthy and The Other Isn't*).
12 Theatre Audience Waiting Room – see 11.
13 Metalwork/Woodwork Room – where pupils are taught to make iron girders and pencils, to help keep the school standing and functioning.
14 Home Economics Room – where pupils are taught to appreciate school food, which is marginally better than their own, but only because they're taught to cook by an ex-dinner lady.
15 Loos – where pupils go to dispose of school food.
16 Bike Sheds – doubling as Sex Education area.
17 Playground – doubling as everything else education area. Also doubling as caretaker's smoking lounge, and dog exercise/feeding area (feeding, that is, if some poor first year happens to be crossing it with a note).
18 Staffroom.
19 Liberal Studies Department – formerly the coal cellar.
20 Equipment/Stationery Room – or rather the room with the old brown paper bag in which the school equipment/stationery is kept.
BUSHES – to keep the prying eyes of parents out.
WIRE FENCE (ELECTRIC) – to keep the pupils in.
GATES – purely ornamental, they haven't worked for years. However, they are very ornate and come in handy for impressing overseas visitors, even if they do have to then climb in through a hole in a bush.

The A-Z of school

A

Amusement arcade

Half your class might be in there on a good day, but this isn't an annexe of your school. In fact it's unlikely that the staff of your school or the school governors have any say at all in the running of the place – unless of course one of them owns it. (*See also* **Governors**.)

Asking

One of the most difficult things at school is asking. Your average mixed infant would rather wet their pants than ask to go to the toilet. Your average junior (or even senior) would rather go ignorant than ask the teacher to explain what they're talking about (assuming they *could*, of course)!

I remember my own first day at secondary school. I was twenty-seven.[1] I had been given a note by the

---

1. I was a late developer. This was partly due to my hobby of looking out of the window, in which I had attained Olympic standards, and partly due to my fear of asking.

woodwork teacher, which I was supposed to deliver to the German teacher.[1] Having a child's natural curiosity,[2] I stopped off at the domestic science room[3] to steam the envelope open. I managed to fool the domestic science teacher that I was carrying out a very important experiment (Watt's Steam Engine theory and its relevance to the British Postal System). She believed me![4] The note revealed that the woodwork teacher was unable to meet the German teacher for a snogging session that breaktime, which was a pity because, as I later discovered, some of the fifth-year boys used to organize sight-seeing trips that took in this particular attraction. Oh, well, their profits would be down that week, and they'd have to go back to bullying! (*See also* **Bullying**.)

Having discovered the contents of the note, I then set out to find the teacher it was intended for. That was the hard part. With hindsight, I should probably have got the school secretary to announce it over the public address system, but you never think of these things at the time, do you? Anyway, that school was impossible to find your way around, or my way around for that matter. Whoever designed it needed shooting, if anyone could ever find him![5]

On my journey I met a little old man with a very long beard. I mistook him for Rumplestiltskin and tried to interest him in doing my homework for me,[6] but it

1. She was English but she taught German. A fact that we all found very suspicious, so soon after the end of World War II.
2. Which, being 27, was not mine. I was renting it on a weekly basis from a much younger boy.
3. Recently renamed the Joan Collins Home Economics Block – rather inappropriately, I feel.
4. But then she had children and pets and a husband and everything, so she couldn't have been a proper teacher, could she?
5. I'm assuming that the architect was a man. Women are usually far too practical to design anything so complex.
6. After all, anyone who can weave straw into gold must be able to do algebra.

turned out that he was a Mixed Infant who had gone in search of the toilet in 1927! I tactlessly suggested that he should have asked someone, but he wouldn't hear of it. In fact, he only allowed me to tell him where it was after he had convinced himself beyond a shadow of doubt that I wasn't a teacher in disguise. This he did by checking that all my clothes were name-tagged,[1] and that there wasn't the slightest hint of chalk dust about my person. We must have looked a very strange sight, but I managed to persuade any passers-by that I was undergoing a school medical, which – due to cutbacks – was taking place in the middle of the playground.

After I had directed him to the lavatory, and he had relieved himself,[2] he explained why it had taken him so long to go: he was afraid to ask. I understood completely. Why, my own journey had taken so long that I had been given forty-seven detentions for missed homework.[3]

As for the German teacher, she was convinced that the woodwork teacher no longer fancied her, having heard nothing from him for so long, so she married a bloke she met at ballroom dancing classes. He stood out from the rest, because he only had one leg. He wasn't a great dancer, but he won a lot of hearts (and sympathy) by falling over.

Why is it that so many of us are frightened to ask questions at school? Is it because we don't want to draw attention to ourselves? After all, when you're at school you mostly want to keep your head down and hope

1. Teachers, don't bother to label their clothes because they never take them off, even to sleep!
2. An event which caused the local weatherman to give a flood warning on the six o'clock news.
3. The fact that my parents didn't notice I was missing did rather upset me, I have to say.

nobody picks on you, don't you? Maybe it relates back to Infant School, when the usual reason for putting your hand up in class was to ask to go to the toilet. Or, more accurately, to ask to be allowed to go to your Thunderbirds peg and get your change of underwear. Is that it? Is it because:

a We don't want the other kids to know our business?[1] I must admit that even as an adult I find it embarrassing to go to the loo on a train, because you have to walk through the carriage and everybody knows where you're going.[2]

b We don't want other kids to think we're thick, even though the last exam results confirmed that none of us was the Brain of Britain?

c We're afraid of embarrassing the teacher, because from past experience, whenever anyone has been brave enough to put up their hand and ask a question, the teacher hasn't known the answer?

Whatever the reason, this fear of asking is a problem. So what is the solution? I hear you cry. You're asking me? I mean, you're actually brave enough to stick your hand up and ask me? Even if everyone around thinks you want to go to the toilet and starts giggling? Well, if you're bold enough to ask, then I hardly think you need my advice on this one, do you?

1. Or rather that we don't want them to know that we want to *do* our business!
2. That plus the fact that if you go to the loo on a train, it always pulls into a station just as you flush the loo, and you then have to decide whether to walk out of the cubicle while the train is stationary and have everyone think you broke the golden rule about not flushing in stations, or to stay in the loo while the train is stopped and have everyone who is waiting wet themselves. Life is riddled with this sort of dilemma.

Avoiding initiation ceremonies

On your first day at Big School, you'll probably find yourself the potential victim of an initiation ceremony. These are referred to earlier in the book, and aren't as terrifying as they may at first appear, if you follow this simple advice. The best form of defence is to stop hiding, step out in the open, and say: "Here I am! I'm ready for you to stick my head down the toilet!" This should make the fifth-years lose interest in you. Oh, all right, it never does, but at least it gets the whole messy business over and done with much more quickly. (*See also* **Bullying**.)

WOULD YOU LIKE A BLINDFOLD?

B

Bike sheds, behind the
Ah, the bike sheds! Memories! Memories! Actually, you couldn't get behind the bike sheds at my old school. They were built against a wall. Some kids tried, of course, but then they were thick. (*See also* **Prefects**.) Not being able to get behind the bike sheds meant that we were denied all those simple, illicit pleasures that can only be experienced there – smoking that first cigarette, swopping that first dirty photo,[1] lying about what you got up to:

1. Which always turned out to be of footballers, fully dressed, in my experience. Maybe we weren't doing it properly.

We missed out on all of that. At least, we did until one teacher realized that being denied the basic right to go behind the bike sheds might stunt our emotional growth and arranged for us to time-share a bike shed with the school up the road. Of course it wasn't the same thing at all. For one thing, it never really felt like our bike shed. The graffiti was very different. They were an all-girls school so there was quite a bit of it that we didn't understand. We thought of asking one of the girls from our school to explain, but we didn't want to appear unworldly. Most of us have probably remained ignorant of the contents of that graffiti to this day – I know I have. Still, it couldn't have been important. I've got by without the need to know. Come to think of it, it was probably Algebra. It gets everywhere!

Bullying

I think we've all come across this one at some time, haven't we? Perhaps even without really realizing that it *was* bullying. Even in infant school you get the bigger kid who says, "Give us a crisp," in such a way that you hand the packet over without a second thought. The bigger kid probably says, "Thanks" as he scoffs your favourite packet of prawn and pickle flavour. Is this bullying? Well, it probably wouldn't be if this bigger kid didn't have half a dozen even bigger (but stupider) kids flanking him and looking menacing – bigger and stupider kids who don't even get a share of the crisps for their trouble, I might add! I suppose the trick is to refuse to be intimidated. Because you know in your heart of hearts that if you hand over the crisps, it'll just go on, getting worse. Today crisps, tomorrow, who knows? A three-course meal? Money? A horse?

"Have a horse here tomorrow or I'll . . . er . . . I'll make you do my homework!"

Well, *I'd* be frightened! But why do some kids bully? And how do they pick their targets? Because there's no doubt that a certain type of kid is a bully while another type gets bullied. I was bullied as a child by a kid who lived in the same street, and all my "friends" joined in on his side. Please don't weep for me – it really wasn't that bad, although of course I thought it was at the time. He was younger than me, and when he started attending the same secondary school, I thought I was really for it. Strangely enough, I met him years later, on a bus. I reminded him about it, and asked him why he had done it. Did he say:

"Don't talk to me like that, or I'll thump yer!"?

No, he didn't! He said he didn't know. And he was very sorry. I forgave him. Now, the odd thing about him was that he was very intelligent (as were all the bullies at my secondary school)[1] and good-looking (as they all were). They all attracted a strong following from other kids who were more than happy to do things for them, just to be their mates. These other kids tended to be a lot less bright/good-looking.

So is this the key? Is your average bully simply demonstrating his power over his followers by picking on someone who seems less impressed by him? I mean, what would you do if, through no fault of your own, you suddenly found that a bunch of half-baked dingbats had elected you leader of their group? Well, you'd be flattered for a start, wouldn't you? Then you'd probably want to hang on to them, wouldn't so? So you'd have to do the occasional deed, just to prove that you were worthy of being called leader. In olden times this was called heroism or chivalry. Today it's called bullying. Because, let's face it, if you're looking around for some

1. OK, so you'll probably argue that it isn't very intelligent to go around threatening people. I really mean academic.

feat to perform to impress your cohorts, a school playground isn't really the ideal place, is it? There are no dragons to slay, no damsels to rescue, and no fierce enemies to see off, so you're stuck with things like cheeking the caretaker or knocking the fat kid's glasses off. And because these tasks are pathetic and ludicrous, you as leader cannot really be seen to do them, so you demonstrate your powers over your followers by telling them to do it. And your followers are over the moon and fall over themselves to do your bidding, stupid and trivial though it may be.

But what's the answer to this problem? Well, hours of television time and acres of book and newspaper print have been devoted to the subject of bullying, all putting forward different theories and offering different solutions. The simple fact is that it's probably just a part of growing up, although some people never grow out of it, and carry on picking on smaller, weaker people for the rest of their lives. To those people I would say, remember that "The meek shall inherit the earth." And, when you're lying on the operating table awaiting that life-saving operation, and notice a strange gleam in the eye of the surgeon as he toys with his scalpel, insist on him lowering his mask and showing you his face. It just might be that squitty little kid from 4B! (*See also* **Extortion with Menaces**.)

Bus, school

You've got to have something seriously wrong with your brain to want to drive a school bus. With this in mind, I sent Elderado Dingbatti along to the job centre to apply for a position as school bus driver as advertised in the window. The post had unexpectedly fallen vacant halfway up the High Street. One moment the driver had been happily chugging along, whistling some tune that had made Rolf Harris a household name, and the next moment the bus was blocking the traffic and all they could find was his cap. What had happened? Who knows? One kid had been heard to complain that he felt hungry, but he was excluded from police enquiries when he told them he was a vegetarian. Anyway, Elderado didn't get the job, even though he had bus-driving experience. He'd once spent a day driving a one-man operated bus, which had crashed. Elderado claimed that it couldn't have been his fault, as he was upstairs collecting fares at the time.

But why are school buses such dangerous places? Well, think about it. Kids spend all day in school, being told what do do, where to go, what to think, etc. Then they go home, where they are told what not to do, where not to go, what not to think, etc. In between these two, they're on the bus! And, let's face it, your average bus driver is too busy watching the road to start telling you how to behave. So as long as nobody gets blood on the seats, why should he worry? It's not his job keeping kids under control, is it? That's the teacher's work, innit? And besides . . . yes! OK, driver! We take your point! Get your eyes back on the road, will you? Oops! Oh, well, I never did like cats, anyway.[1]

---

1. Not true! I love cats! (Just in case there are any cats reading this book.)

C

Caretakers
(See under **Cleaner-in-charge.***)*

Chewing gum
See under your desk-lid.

Cleaner-in-charge
In some areas this is the current title for what used to be called a school caretaker. In the past all schools had someone to literally "take care" of the school in every respect: heating, lighting, leaky taps, faulty teachers, etc. Now, in these times of cut-backs, anything faulty stays that way, including the teachers. But at least they're clean.[1] Because that's what a cleaner-in-charge is: a *cleaner* in charge. In charge of what? Well, in the bigger school, they'll be in charge of other cleaners. In tiny schools they'll be in charge of a bucket. Not that that's an easy job! Oh, no! Buckets can be pretty tricky things. They can fill up with water in no time, for instance, especially if you put them under a tap. They can empty pretty sharpish too, if you kick them over.

Of course, the cleaner-in-charge of a very large school might be called upon to make several difficult decisions every day. For instance, which corner of the carpet in the TV/video room to hide the dust under this week, and whether to bother to sweep the floor at all. (After all, there isn't much point. It'll only get dirty again, when the kids start standing on it.) Then he has to decide whether to have a tea break before, after or instead of work. It's a hard life!

You can hardly blame the poor cleaner-in-charge for

1. The schools, not the teachers, although some teachers really do scrub up quite nicely. Almost presentable.

this change in his circumstances. They don't have the power that caretakers had in the past. Why, old Mr Hemeroid, the caretaker at my last school, could clean a window so well that no-one was allowed to breathe in that room for a week.[1] He could polish a floor so brightly that an entire gym class could slip and break their necks before they even got to the wall bars. But then he had the training. He had come from a long line of Hemeroids who had been school caretakers man, boy and unpleasant-looking space alien for generations. The true art of school caretaking had been handed down to him in a leather-bound, blood-proof handbook. Our own dear A.J. Gruntwick (RN Retired), caretaker of this parish, tried to get a look at the book, but it self-destructed as he opened it, leaving him with a blackened face, hurt pride, and a huge bill for damage to the Singing Tarzan-O-Gram costume he had hired in order to get him into the *Bideawee But Wipeyefeet Resthome For Extremely Unpleasant Old Caretakers*, where

Hemeroid is living out his last days, dreaming up even more devious ways of torturing children now that he has been forbidden by law to come within four thousand kilometres of them. Oh, if only we could have viewed that book! It would all have been in there. All the old craftsman's skills, lost forever!

1. He certainly did his bit for classroom overcrowding.

Of course, you can still find the odd caretaker lurking in a cupboard, blissfully unaware that progress has made him redundant. Rather like a very old Japanese soldier lurking in the jungles of the South Pacific, totally unaware that the war is over. There he crouches, highly trained and highly polished,[1] just waiting to pounce. So beware, because one day you may be walking along the school corridor, minding your own business the way you do, when suddenly – boing! He'll leap out on you, bash you over the head with his broom handle, and yell: "Gerroff my parquet floorin'!" And that's just the Japanese soldier!

Crushes

Anyone who says they've never had a school crush is lying. Mind you, by the same token, half the people who say they *have* are lying too.[2] What I'm basically trying to say is that everyone's had a school crush, except those who haven't. Clear now? Good! Either way, I'm sure we all know what I'm talking about, don't we? Yes! The Agony and the Ecstasy. You feel hot and cold, you can't breathe, can't think straight . . . or is that exams? It's probably both. And who's making you feel like this? That little blonde in 3C? That big footballing hunk in 5A? The cleaner's dog? Not usually. If it was any of

1. So highly polished that he can see his face in himself.
2. If that doesn't make mathematical sense, don't worry. I was away when they did maths.

these I'm sure something could be worked out.[1] But, no. Usually the object of your passion is one of the teachers. How hopeless can true love get?

It isn't even as though you get any warning, is it? You've barely noticed this particular teacher. They're just another grotesque blot on the landscape of your youth. Then one day, when they're unhooking you from the wall bars where you've been left as part of some outmoded school ritual, your eyes meet, and . . . *ding*! Or *boing*! Or *ferkang*! Or whatever noise crush-love makes. You're in love!

"Run along," says Teacher.

"Ah!", you sigh, because you know they don't actually mean that. What they actually mean is, "Run a long slim hand through my hair and call me Sexy-Boots," because they're in love with you too, although they haven't realized yet and probably never will, but that's one of the great complexities of crush-love. How was it that Shakespeare put it? I'm not sure, but he got his face slapped a few times.

Anyway, having fallen hopelessly in love and knowing that Teacher feels exactly the same, although he/she is (very cleverly) showing no outer signs of this, you proceed to make a complete idiot of yourself, don't you? Ah, the things we do for love! Try to find out what Teacher's first name is, so that you can scratch out *Jason Donovan* from the desk lid and replace him with your new love's name.[2] Strap your skateboard to the back of Teacher's battered VW, so that you can follow him/her back to the Hideous Green Slimepit that all teachers return to at night. And what are you going to do when you get there? Hang around outside? What? Well, in the spirit of true love you haven't actually thought that far

1. Except possibly with the dog, but then he's always been a terrible flirt.
2. And that's just the lads!

ahead. But that's the way it gets you. You find yourself doing little things, like leaving strange objects on the edge of Teacher's desk, which always seem to get knocked accidentally into the wastepaper basket before they're spotted. But it doesn't matter, you'll do anything to please Teacher. Of course the things that would really please never occur to you – things like getting on with your work, paying attention and doing your homework. But then true love transcends such mundane things.

Of course, this kind of relationship is doomed from the start, whatever lengths you go to to plan everything carefully. Imagine the situation. It's the night of the school disco (*see* **School discos**). You've concocted some convoluted plan, involving the Bomb Squad, Jeremy Beadle and the entire cast of *Neighbours*, that should result in you being left alone with Teacher.[1] Your plan is

1. This plan had better work, since it's costing you six years' pocket money!

basically this: at the crucial moment, when you've manoeuvred Teacher into a dark corner, Spotty Wellsbury[1] will rush into the hall and shout: "Quick, everyone! Come outside! The cast of *Neighbours* are blowing up Jeremy Beadle!"[2]

You feel sure your plan will work, because your extensive research has shown you that Teacher can't stand Jeremy Beadle.[3] And your plan probably *would* work, except that at the golden moment, Teacher turns and says, "I don't believe you've met my wife/husband, have you?"!

Aaagh! No! Oh, well, better stick to people your own age or younger. First-years can be persuaded quite easily to let you have crushes on them. (*See* **Bullying**.)

A word of advice, however. Having a crush always involves writing the name of the object of your desire on the cover of your exercise book. And, since the available space on an exercise book is limited, make sure the crush is going to last long enough for you to write the name![4]

1. Bribed easily for only 50p. Anyone interested please note.
2. Actually, it'll be the bomb squad doing the blowing up. The cast of *Neighbours* can't even handle dialogue, let along high explosives.
3. In fact Teacher can't stand practical jokes of any sort, having once been a victim of one. Teacher went into the classroom one April the First, only to be greeted by the sight of the entire fifth form roasting an ox. Even though they all yelled "April Fool!" Teacher never got over the experience, and is a vegan to this day, wearing plastic shoes that make their feet sweat. The smell hung in the air for months. The ox, that is, not the feet.
4. The same applies to desk lids.

D

Dancing, country

As I mentioned earlier, I have first-hand experience of the horrors of country dancing, and firmly believe it was invented by a particularly warped teacher. If you don't believe me, go and watch the country dancing display next time your local junior school has a fête or open day. As those poor little kids are stripping the willow, dosey-do-ing or whatever else they do, watch the teachers. Why are they all writhing around on the floor like that?[1] They can't all have some incurable twitching disease, can they? No, of course not! They're laughing uncontrollably. And they can hardly believe that you've all fallen for it. Every time they stick on those country

1. Ignore Ms Pentel and Mr Boggly. They've just got engaged, so they don't count.

dance records – *The Gay Gordons* and so forth – they
hesitate, expecting the entire dance team to say, "This is
rubbish!" But amazingly, they never do. They just bow
to their partners and start skipping around the room,
plimsoles squeaking and bums sticking out. You can't
really blame the teachers for laughing. After all, they
don't get a lot of fun in their lives, do they?

Dinner ladies

There are certain kinds of food it's impossible to cook
badly, unless you're specially trained in that art. This is

what happens in the case of dinner ladies. I know this for
a fact, because my mother was a dinner lady years ago,
and she's a pretty good cook at home. Her dinner lady
past is something she doesn't really like to broadcast,
and I'm sure she won't thank me for telling you now.

This is probably because she's been reliably informed
that one ex-pupil has taken a contract out on her, even
though it wasn't her fault and she was only following
orders.

Actually, I'm not sure they're still called dinner ladies.
I think they're called lunchtime supervisors, or something that suggests they've got nothing whatsoever to do
with the cooking process.[1] Wise ladies. After all, they
don't buy the food, they just stand helplessly by as meat
and veg turn into a browny-green liquid. Then they add
glue to try and keep it on the plates. So don't blame them
– they're trying their best! (*See* **Meals, School**.)

1. This was a ruling insisted on by the dinner ladies' union – Supervisors,
Lunch Operatives and Personnel (SLOP) – after several of their members fell
victim to playground lynch mobs.

Discos, school

If you've ever been to a real disco (which I'm sure most of you have), you'll know that there's no such thing as a school disco. It's just country dancing with the lights off. Not even off, really – just covered in coloured stuff to make them dimmer.[1] Of course, the teachers very generously provide the records, but you can't honestly be expected to listen to Abba all night[2], can you! Mind you, these events don't normally go on all night. After all, you've got school in the morning, as the teacher in charge keeps reminding you while the caretaker beats the boys and girls apart with a broom handle. What's his problem? You're not doing anything! You're not even in the same room! Next time they offer you a disco, ask for extra homework instead!

1. To match some of the dancers.
2. Well, all night is a bit of an exaggeration. Until 10.30p.m.

E

Extortion with menaces

This is another, far more sinister, form of bullying. What it basically involves is someone (the bully) asking someone else (the bullied) if they could lend them some money, please, without being in too much of a hurry to get it back. The bullied readily agrees, due to the presence of a large number on onlookers (thugs). This situation continues until the first person becomes very rich, the second person very poor, and the thugs . . . well, they just stay stupid really. Which is rather unfair in a way, because they sort of do all the work, although of course they never realize this. (*See* **Bullying**.)

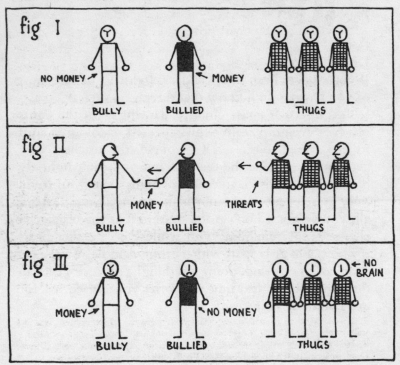

F

Football, school

Try this experiment: Get hold of anything that is evil-smelling and disgusting-looking, tie it to the end of a piece of string and swing it round your head,[1] making sure that the string is long enough to ensure that the object clears any sticking-out bits of your body.[2] Make sure also that it is tied on tight enough. You don't really want it to fly off and hit anyone.[3] In no time at all you should have attracted the attention of any flies in the area.[4] Once you have achieved this, try changing the direction of the swing. Dip it. Make it swoop. You will discover that the flies will follow it with fervour, no matter how frustrated they may get that they can't catch it. This experiment will illustrate perfectly and graphically the nature of school football. Imagine that the object at the end of the string is a football, and the flies are the players. Next time you watch a game of school football, notice how everyone – players, goalies, ref., bystanders, pensioners walking their dogs – rushes after the ball. Often they do this with such enthusiasm that

1. Don't be tempted to use your smaller brother. Even though he may fit the bill as regards smell and appearance.
2. Especially your nose!
3. If you do, then that is a completely different type of experiment which I will try to cover in some future book. (Look out for *Coping With Families*.)
4. It is a fly's lot in life to seek out evil-smelling things, and walk all over them, before gate-crashing picnics and walking all over the sandwiches.

they don't even notice when they get near the goal mouth, so the score is usually nil-nil.

But still, everyone has a good time, and gets plenty of exercise, and that's what football's all about, isn't it?

Free meals

Some school pupils are allowed free school meals because their parents are on income support. I think this is very unfair. If one's parents are short of money through no fault of their own, it's adding insult to injury to make their child eat school dinners. After all, what have they ever done to anyone? (*See* **Meals, School.**)

G

Games

An essential part of your education, they'd like you to believe. Don't! It's just another way teachers have of amusing themselves. You may not find slopping through mud on a cross-country run or trying to play netball in a Force 9 gale the least bit amusing, but then you're not sitting in the games hut, warming your hands on an oil stove and watching through the window.

Governors, school

In these times of great change in the way schools are run and financed, a strong school Governing body has never been more important. They make all the major decisions that affect the smooth running of the school, such as whether the school should pay for biscuits in the staffroom, or whether the teachers should bring some in from home.

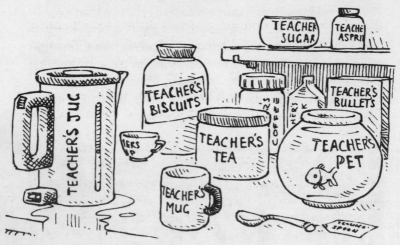

In an Appendix at the back of the book, I have reprinted (at great personal risk to myself) the minutes of a meeting of school govenors, smuggled out by one of my research team, Miss Prim, who managed to enter the school disguised as an escaped lunatic – a part she played with frightening realism. A governors' meeting was convened while she sat shackled to the radiator waiting for the men in white coats. For a moment it looked as if the game was up. One of the governors objected to her presence, as the meeting was confidential. The quick-thinking Miss Prim, although almost overcome by the heat of the radiator as it was June (*see* **Radiator Day**), pointed out that, as an ex-pupil of the school, she was unlikely to understand a word of what the governors were saying. This seemed to satisfy them, and an edited transcript of this meeting appears at the end of the book.

H

Homework

This is the work you are given to do at home because there wasn't time to do it in class, probably because someone was talking – usually the teacher. Homework falls into two categories:

1) Long, hard, boring stuff that no-one can understand.
2) Long, hard, boring stuff that's of no earthly use to anyone anyway.

So why do teachers bother to give it to you? Is it to stop you watching *Beadle's About*? Or is there a deeper, more sinister reason? Personally, I plump for the latter, but only because I'm not a Jeremy Beadle fan. So what is this deeper, more sinister reason? I'll tell you – parents.

Consider this. Who helps you when you're stuck on your homework, and generally gets it wrong? That's right – Mum and Dad, collectively known as parents. Do you think your teachers don't know this? Of course they do! By giving you homework, they aren't testing you, they're testing your parents! Yeah! They're checking up to see if your parents can remember anything *they* were taught at school. But why do teachers need this information? Well, I would have thought that was obvious. They want to be fore-armed, in case your mum and dad go up to the school to complain. After all, if your mum does your homework badly, and then goes into school to complain about the way you're being taught, the teacher can just turn round and say, "What would *you* know about it!"

Sneaky, eh? But you can beat them at their own game. "How?" I hear you say.

"Easily," I reply. "Do your homework *yourself*!" That'll show 'em! Mind you, your parents will probably still get the blame, but then that's school, I'm afraid!

I

Inter-house rivalry

The same applies to inter-house rivalry. Some schools are divided into houses. They're usually named after famous dead people that no-one really gives a stuff about, like Shelley, Wordsworth, etc., but the more adventurous school might plump for naming their houses after African leaders.

My old school was really controversial. The houses there were called Red, Blue, Yellow, and . . . erm . . . Cerise,[1] which was fine for everyone except colour-blind illiterates.[2] The stupid thing about this system was that you were allotted to houses the minute you set foot in the school, long before the teachers got to know you or recognize your many abilities. Consequently all the geniuses, sports and otherwise were in Red, and all the "dregs"[3] were – you've guessed it – with me! But we did our best, and when the call came to "come forth", we did – we came fourth.

Many of us[4] questioned the purpose of this inter-house rivalry. What was the point of it? Was it meant to be character-building? If so, it did absolutely nothing for me! Was it meant to teach us to survive in an increasingly competitive world? I don't think so. It's my belief that the sole purpose of the house system was to amuse the teachers. Let's face it, they don't get a lot to laugh at, apart from each other.

1. Guess which house they stuck me in?
2. And anyone in Cerise House.
3. Not that we considered ourselves dregs. We simply held the opinion that there was more to life than being good at things.
4. The whole of Cerise, anyway.

Inter-school rivalry

I've always thought this was a waste of time, but I suppose you'll never stop the kids from another school jostling you in the bus queue and saying, "Your school's rubbish!"

Yes. So? Why is he bothering to tell you something you've known for ages? And how are you supposed to react? Be amazed? Offended? Sensing that he has the

advantage, he then follows up with: "Our school's better than your school!"

Hang on! If we've already established that your school's rubbish, a fact that you haven't disputed as far as you know, why is he bothering to say that his school's better? Better than rubbish? That's not saying a lot really, is it? It seems to me that it would make far more sense to be arguing about which school was *worse*, not better. Now that *is* worth arguing about!

J

Janitor
See under **Cleaner-in-charge**.

Janitor, where to find the dead
See under the flowerbed by the corner of the Science Block.

K

Kit, games
Providing games kit is compulsory. It's also very expensive, which is probably why your mum gets cross when you accidentally come home without yours, but less cross if you accidentally come home with someone else's, especially if theirs is newer. But just because it's expensive, don't assume that everyone who does gym in their underwear is necessarily poor. It could be that they want you to have a crush on them. (*See also* **Crushes**.)

Kitchens, school

The most unsuitably-named building on the planet.[1] Oh, yes, it may be full of kitchen equipment, it may even have people standing around looking like cooks, but that's where any similarity to the real thing ends. After all, food comes out of a real kitchen, but food poisoning is the only thing that comes out of your average school kitchen. It's the only room that has a sign saying "Please wash your hands before you use the toilet."

I've heard it said that if you were to visit a pork pie factory, you'd never eat a pork pie again. Well, if you visited a school kitchen, you'd never eat *anything* again! That's always assuming you got out alive! Because, as you probably know, they'll put anything in a school dinner. You can't really blame the cooks[2]. After all, they're only trying to give the food a bit of flavour. But it does explain why so many things go missing in schools. Why there are never any pencils. Why most kids have only got one gym trainer. Why Mycroft never came back from delivering that note. You were told he'd been abducted by aliens, weren't you? Well, it's far more likely that he met his fate closer to home, and that you probably had a share in his misfortune – unless of course you take a packed lunch! (*See also* **Packed lunch, notes.**)

1. Except possibly "British Rail Enquiries".
2. Unless you want to end up stuffed!

L

Learning

It's generally accepted that "A little learning is a dangerous thing." If this is so, why do politicians, who are meant to be intelligent,[1] make us do about twelve years of it?

OH NO! HERE COMES DANGEROUS-DOUG, HE'S HAD MORE YEARS OF LEARNING THAN ANYONE!

M

Meals, school

By meals, I am of course referring to that stuff they put on plates in the dining hall round about lunchtime. Of course these have changed greatly over the years. At one time a school dinner consisted of a mountain of cabbage, slightly higher than Everest. They used to leave the slugs in, as there was a meat shortage. These days more and more children are taking packed lunches. That way at least the police know who to question if it kills you. Similarly, a lot of kids go to the chip shop or burger bar at lunchtime.

---

1. I'm not sure that all politicians realize this.

The school meals people became aware of this trend
some time ago, and began a real effort to make school
meal times more attractive. They took the chains off the
plates for a start, then they did away with the Ninja
monitors and the big bloke with the whip who makes
you eat your swede.[1] They brightened the hall up and

1. Swede is one of those vegetables that you only ever come across on a
school dinner plate. I think it was specially created. The question is, what
from?

laid on entertainers like jugglers and clowns.[1] None of this worked. Then some bright spark said, "If the kids are all going to the burger bar, why don't we offer them burgers?" So they did. They provided exactly the same food that the local burger bar was doing, at a much lower price. That should work, surely? It didn't. Why not? Because it still tasted like sawdust.

1. They really should have laid on food-testers, but they couldn't find anyone brave enough.

N

National curriculum

This is far, far too complicated to explain, but I can tell you how it came into being. A minor civil servant in the Department of Education and Science[1], waiting for the 17.23 to Surbiton one evening, overheard a teacher telling a colleague, "I spent the whole of last summer holidays touring the Greek islands!" The civil servant was immediately green with envy, and decided to get his own back. I've always said those long holidays were a mistake.

Nits

Or, to give them their proper names, Norman and Nora Nit. (Only joking.)[2]

The proper name is of course head lice. They probably have a Latin name, something like *Licus Hedus*, I expect. Anyway, they're a pain. By that, I don't actually mean that they hurt. In fact, they only start itching after they've been living in your hair for some months.[3] They're just really tricky to get rid of. You have to use special shampoo or lotion, which is particularly irritat-

1. They obviously think science and education are two separate things!
2. Yes! Honestly! It was a joke! You can laugh if you like! Oh, please yourself!
3. I don't know about you, but my head's starting to itch just thinking about them.

ing if you don't like washing your hair in the first place! In fact, why not stop washing your hair altogether or shave your head? Because nits only like clean hair – a fact that the various Health Authorities have gone completely overboard to try and tell people.

Having nits is still a bit like being a leper.[1] Your mum would rather have you go to school with a paper bag on your head, or stay away completely, than let it be known that you've got nits. The silly thing is that it's much better to know if anyone's got nits so that it can be treated, because it spreads really fast. How does it

LIKE I SAY NORA YOU'VE GOT TO GET A HEAD IN LIFE

1. Except bits of your body don't fall off, at least only in very extreme cases.

spread? They crawl from head to head. In fact some time ago the government were so worried about the spread of nits that they brought in a ruling preventing teachers from banging pupil's heads together. This was because nits were so intelligent that they knew when this was going to happen and took the opportunity to move on[1]

So what can you do about them? Get them treated immediately, and insist that the rest of your family use the special shampoo as well. Oh, and if you know that there are nits in the school,[2] I suggest that you don't get your head too close to anyone else's. (*See* **Bike Sheds, behind the.**)

Nit nurse (Latin name: *Nitti Nora*)
Although nits are not a thing of the past, the nit nurse is.[3] She's a victim of financial cuts, along with everything else that's fun.

"The nit nurse – fun?" I hear you say.

Yes! Just think of it. An hour of lessons missed while you line up and have a nurse run her fingers through your hair. Nothing to it. OK, so there is always the possibility that she might find a nit, but at least you don't have to do sums! Actually, I suppose the worst thing that could happen is that you line up, completely nitless, and then some nit-infested Clean-Head further up the line allows one of his nits to crawl on to the nurse's hand, where it waits until you come along then crawls on to your head. Just your luck! Why do they never crawl on to the bully's head? Too frightened, I suppose.

1. Some teachers are still rather annoyed that this particular form of punishment has never been replaced.
2. The little crawly ones, I mean, not the big stupid ones who follow bullies around.
3. In many areas, anyway.

Anyway, in the absence of a genuine nit nurse with all the certificates, badges, special hat, etc., who checks for nits? The answer is nobody (although some caretakers have offered to do it with weed-killer), which is presumably why nits are still so common. You see, my research shows that teachers aren't allowed to check heads for nits because this could be considered as singling a child out for ridicule. Does that sound right to you? After all, if nits only like clean hair, where's the social stigma?

Notes

A large amount of communication in schools is done via notes. This is why teachers get you to read and write so quickly – so that you'll be able to join in the note-writing.

There are notes from parents to teachers. These usually explain why you haven't been to school. They are sometimes forged. Then there are notes from school to home. These usually cover events such as school holidays, special school events, ceremonial Burning of the School Tea-Towel – that sort of thing. These are usually genuine, although I suppose there would be nothing to stop you forging one if you could think of a really good event to tell your parents that the school was holding. For instance:

Dear Parent,

This is to let you know that the school will be holding a fund-raising event later in the term. This will take the form of an Over-Sixties Olympics. If your child has an old granny or grandpa who's just sitting around doing nothing, preferably one that isn't afraid of heights, fire or mud, just fill their names in on the attached form(with out telling them might be best) and send it in to the school secretary before the end of the month. We would also like to provide your old people with life insurance, as this could also be a way to raise money for the school.

Yours Faithfully,

T. Drinker (HEAD TEACHER)[1]

1. Head*case* by the sound of it!

Yes! This is the sort of note you could forge, and I think you'd be amazed just how many people would turn up with their old folks. Try it![1]

Other kinds of note are the ones passed from pupil to pupil, teacher to teacher, teacher to pupil, pupil to teacher. Some of these concern school matters, and some involve *love*! (*See also* **Crushes**.) The trick is to be able to tell the difference. If, for instance, your favourite teacher sends you a note asking you to go to the stationery cupboard, and lists the items you are to fetch, chances are that next time they see you they'll expect you to have armfuls of pens and pencils, not flowers and chocolates. On the other hand, if the note says "I think you're wonderful! Meet me in the stationery cupboard!" ... well, it's probably a forgery! Sorry about that! But let's face it, no teacher is going to risk their career, not to mention risk getting prodded in the backside by a box of pencils, by meeting their favourite pupil in the stationery cupboard.

Here are a few hints about forging notes:

1 Don't use too many long words. If the note is meant to be from your parents, use the sorts of words they use.[2] First make sure your parents can spell. In fact you'd better make sure they can actually write, because if they can't the note will be a bit of a waste of time!

2 Keep the note simple and to the point. If you're pretending to be ill, just put "so-and-so won't be in school today because he/she has a cold." Don't give your medical history. Chances are that the teacher will only glance at it vaguely anyway. If the note is too long, this might arouse their suspicion.

---

1. Maybe not!
2. Ones that are printable in a note, that is!

114

3 Don't try and cover your tracks – there's no need. By this I mean don't put something like: "So-and-so won't be in school today because they're having their leg off. However, they might hop down to the amusement arcade later, just to get a bit of fresh air!" After all, if your teacher happens to see you down at the amusement arcade later, with your full complement of legs, chances are they'll have forgotten that you're meant to have had major surgery that very day.

4 If the note is meant to be from your mum, make sure you use her proper name, and don't put "my mum".

5 And finally, don't refer to yourself in the forged note as "So-and-so", unless of course this is your actual name!

NOTES AND WHERE THEY GO

O

Open day

Much the same as an open evening, only you don't need the lights on.

Open evenings

These usually happen about once a term, and may be the only time some parents realize where their child is going every day. Even then it's often quite difficult to drag parents along. Now, this might strike you as unfair. You might think they're being very lazy,[1] but try to see it from their point of view. What are you asking them to do? Go into a school – a place they left some years earlier, vowing never to go near it again. They might even have left it with the headmaster vowing never to *let* them go there again. Whatever the case, as they walk through those gates, all the memories of school come flooding back. Usually they're not good memories. Sometimes they're the stuff of nightmares! But your parent is prepared to do this for you, for love.[2] The worst thing you're asking your parents to do is to talk to your teacher. Even worse than that, ask your teacher

1. They probably are!
2. Or money, if you've had the good sense to bribe them.

questions! (*See also* **Asking**.) Questions about you! So, before you put your parents through this ordeal, consider these points:

Are you going to like the answers to the questions you're expecting your parents to put to your teacher? More important, are your parents going to like the answers? Because if they don't chances are they'll find a way to make sure that you don't like them either. So, before you rush home with that note inviting your parents to an open evening, weigh up the possible outcome. It could be that a forged note is safer all round – something along the lines of:

Dear Mr and Mrs Dogthrottler.
There will not be the usual open evening this term
Should you see hundreds of your fellow parents
walking towards the school on 15th June at 7.30p.m.
don't worry. They're probably only being abducted
by aliens.
Yours, etc.

Opting out
This is a much discussed recent development in British schools. What it basically means in theory is that school governors can opt to control the school's budget, rather than the local authority. What this means in practice is that if you haven't got a pencil, it's now the head-teacher's fault.

P

Photo, school

Some schools don't bother at all these days, but many realize that not only is the school photo a necessary part of school life, it is also a great way to make money.

Photo sessions can be expensive for a school to set up, though. My research team heard of one school that could only afford to take the photo with one of those disposable cameras. You know the kind of thing, it's really just a film inside a cardboard box. Unfortunately you can't fit many people in the photo. The Head Teacher got around this problem, however, by having a quiet word with the school dinner staff the day before the photo. This meant that most of the pupils were off school with food poisoning, and so those that were left all got in the photo.

One of the most popular types of school photo is still the big long one, with the whole school arranged in rows and the staff plonked in the middle. This obviously requires a very wide angle lens. In the days before such a lens was available, the photographer had to use a special camera that swivelled, photographing each pupil as it passed them. Pupils had to keep still for a very long time.[1] This method is still used, and the great thing about it is that you can get on the picture twice! Make sure you're on the end of the group, and once the camera has passed you, run round and get on the other end.[2] The illustration is of my own school photo. I should point out the Head Master tried the old food poisoning scam, which reduced the number of kids turning up to be snapped. Unfortunately, the photo is still long because most of the school had the idea of getting on both ends of the photo.

1. Something that some schoolkids find really tricky. We heard of one school that used to just take lots of separate photos and stick them all together with sticky tape.
2. Make sure you get put on the end of the group that the camera starts at, otherwise you won't be in the photo at all – twice!

Play, school

The school play is, in theory, a wonderful opportunity for pupils to experience first-hand the skill of the classic dramatist. In practice, however, it's a golden opportunity to get your own back on the boring old bloke for writing the thing in the first place!

Playground

This is where the real lessons are learned if you're going to survive school. Your average playground is like a bazaar,[1] where you can acquire footballing skills by watching the good players, knowledge by talking to the kid in the corner with the book, and peanut butter and tuna sandwiches by bullying the little kids. Mind you, I wouldn't advise this, because you don't know where they've been[2].

The other great thing about a playground is that it's the one place you can be sure a teacher won't venture without a bullet-proof vest. The only real threats to your freedom in the playground are the teacher in the upper window with the Kalashnikov rifle (but he's a lousy shot), the spies who report back if you're spotted doing anything that's not on the National Curriculum (*see* **National Curriculum**) and the prefects (*see* **Prefects**).

1. Perhaps that should read "Your average playground is bizarre."
2. This applies to the sandwiches *and* the little kids!

But apart from genocidal teachers, spies and prefects (and unforeseen circumstances such as invading armies and plagues of frogs), the playground is really the only place you can safely claim as your own, where you can truly be yourself. Although after a few hours of lessons, it's often difficult to know exactly who you are any more, which probably explains why playgrounds seem to be full of people rolling around on the ground in pairs. They're not fighting, although the spies will probably swear that they were and the prefects will shout at them.[1] What they're actually doing is trying to discover their true identities by reading the back of each other's vests!

1. And the teacher on duty will cower further down inside his bullet-proof vest.

Prefects

They look almost human (if a bit train-spottery), but they're not. They were once, of course, but something happens to them when they become a prefect. I never was one, so I've no idea what it is. There may be some strange ceremony involving trouser-rolling, larks' livers and brain-washing,[1] or perhaps there's a drug on the pin of their badge. Who knows? Whatever the reason, they go into the headteacher's office a non-prefect and come out as Terminator II.

HASTA LA VISTA CRY BABY!

After that, they're the only ones brave[2] enough to venture out on to the playground among the real pupils and tell people off. They're fearless! They don't bat an eyelid[3] as they march right up to the biggest bully in the school and tell him his tie's crooked! Wow! And he says: "Sorry!" and straightens it!

1. That's probably why I never became one. I expect they realized I'd never survive the washing.
2. Or stupid.
3. Perhaps they haven't got any eyelids. I've never been close enough to find out.

What kind of stuff are they made of?[1] It's amazing! Even the prime minister doesn't command that kind of respect, though maybe he's a bad example. Prefects! I take my hat off to them. Well, you have to, otherwise you wind up in detention.

Prize giving

This is a special day when everyone in school forgets their private feuds[2] and gathers to praise the great and the good. Freshly scrubbed pupils have their names called out, go up on to the platform and receive some well-deserved prize to thunderous applause. Meanwhile you sit in your seat staring at these victorious hard workers and thinking: "Who *are* these kids? Why have I never seen them in school?"

The fact is, they've probably been hired from some organisation called Rent-A-Swot, just to make you all feel bad.

1. That would make an interesting experiment for your next biology lesson.
2. Even the headteacher starts talking to the staff!

Q

Quiet

This is some teachers' answer to everything, isn't it? You know the scene. You're having a really interesting lesson[1], you actually feel you're learning something,[2] and then – just because somebody makes the mistake of asking a question – the teacher suddenly explodes, going,

"QUIET! I DON'T WANT TO HEAR ANOTHER SOUND!"

It works. Instant silence. The teacher continues:

"Right. That's better. Now, who can tell me the capital of France?"

Total silence, only partially created by hardly anyone knowing the answer.

"Come on!" says Teacher. "It's not that difficult! What's the matter with you?"

A feeble hand goes up.

"You said you didn't want to hear another sound, sir."

"I DIDN'T MEAN LITERALLY!"

Teachers are weird!

1. OK, slightly less boring.
2. Yeah, sorry! I've gone over the top now.

R

Radiator day

I don't know whether you're aware of this, but there's a special day when school radiators are turned on, and obviously there's another one when they're turned off again. These are probably called *Radiator Day*. And on these days the radiators go on or off, whatever the weather. It doesn't matter if your school is in the grip of a freak tropical heatwave – on come the radiators, causing lethal levels of heat-stroke. And if the school is suddenly plunged into a three-metre snow drift, hard luck! The radiators are going off, even though half the class die of frostbite. Why? Well, it wouldn't be unreasonable to assume that this is all due to somebody

WINTER   SUMMER

in the local education office lacking the imagination to make the radiator timetable more flexible, would it? But if you thought that, you'd be wrong. To find out the real reason, you only have to stand outside the boiler-room on Radiator Day and listen to the cackling! (*See also* **Cleaner-in-charge**.)

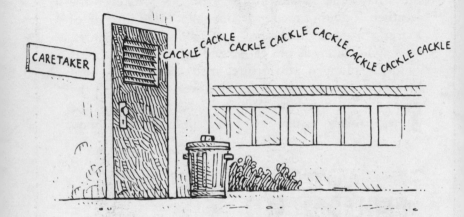

Recorders
Several features of school life have no place in the real world. Algebra is one, recorders another. The dreadful noise that is such a feature of school concerts, especially in primary schools, would be much more bearable if Schubert had written a recorder concerto, or there was a "Handel's Messiah for recorder and fat kid with triangle". But no. Even the rock world has shunned this sad little instrument. Check the inlay cards on any of your tapes or CDs and see if a single one lists a line-up such as: *Wha-Wha Guitar, Steel Pedal Guitar, Heavy Metal Bass, Drums, Programming, and Recorder*. It just doesn't happen!

Rules, school

School rules are so many and various, and change so often, that no-one can possibly keep up with them if they're expected to pay attention in class as well. So what's the solution? Simple! Just assume that anything you plan on doing is wrong.[1] That way you can't get told off, can you? Well, that's the theory, anyway!

1. You can probably breathe, though I would check with a prefect first, just to be on the safe side.

S

Sex education

Teaching sex in school has always been a ticklish subject.[1] After all, it's a very private thing and not everyone wants to talk about it. It puts the teachers in a difficult position. If they appear to know too much or too little about it, it throws up all sorts of speculation about their private lives. And of course the subject makes people giggle. However, I suppose schools will always feel an obligation to teach it, although I think it's unlikely that there'll ever be an exam in it – not a practical one, anyway!

Speech day

Speech days, particularly your first one, are something of a landmark in your time at school. You get to see a famous Old Boy (or Girl), who has usually achieved little apart from staying out of prison.[2] There are lots of speeches, naturally, which is what makes Speech Day different from Prize-giving, although in some schools they are the same thing, and yet again the same few kids get all the prizes. Who are they? How do they find time to get so clever? Don't they ever go home or something? Maybe that's it! They all live in a cupboard and are fed on school dinners. They certainly look undernourished and starved of sunlight. You feel quite sorry for them until you see the size of their cup and hear about the size of their book token. Well, you're not too worried about that. After all, there's one big drawback with book tokens, isn't there? You have to buy books with them.

Speech day is also the day when you learn a great truth

1. If it's too ticklish, then you're probably not doing it right.
2. Which is an achievement in itself.

about your school. No, I'm not referring to the discovery that half the staff like to parade around in their university gowns, while the other half spit because they haven't got any. I'm referring to the fact that you discover, for the very first time, that your school has got a really, really stupid school song, and you're all expected to sing it!

Sports day

The one day of the year when everybody, including the teachers, does exactly as they please, while the headteacher shouts to be heard through a really bad public address system (built in the lunch hour[1] by that swotty kid whose only claim to fame is blowing up the Physics lab), the prefects all walk around with stopwatches, and a couple of sporty kids win all the cups.

1. Well, it was either build a public address system or eat school food.

T

Teaching

Teaching isn't as simple as it looks, unlike teachers, who are more so.

Teams, picking

This must surely rate as one of the great tortures of school. All of you stand freezing on the soccer (or netball) pitch while the two best players pick their teams. They always start with incredible enthusiasm, don't they? You can hear the annoyance in their voices as yet another of their favourites goes to the other side. The voice then changes as they get to the people who could never really call themselves players but at least seem keen and know what the ball looks like (more or less). The voice changes slightly again as we get on to the people who can't play at all but have some sort of novelty value (i.e. they're so fat that they're likely to have a heart attack halfway through the game and push it into extra time). Then, finally, all emotion drains from the voice as we get down to the last six (it's usually six) – the kids who have no redeeming features in the eyes of our two captains of sport. These six are usually great people, often with a wonderful sense of humour.[1] Slowly the team captains pick them with all the enthusiasm of gladiators faced with a choice between arming themselves with a balloon or a stuffed vole.[2] "Smelly" "Snotty" "Dopey" "Sneezy" "Bashful" "Doc . . ."

Hang on! This isn't *Snow White and the Seven Dwarfs*! All I can say to any would-be team captain is this: beware the Last Six, you may need them one day.

1. You have to have one to survive this ordeal.
2. No problem! You can do a lot of damage with a stuffed vole, as long as surprise is on your side.

U

Uniform, school

The great uniform debate goes on and on. Some schools have opted out, and their pupils are already turning up to school dressed in real clothes.[1] The argument *for* wearing uniform is that it looks very smart, and it's nice to be identified with one's school. Wrong! It rarely looks smart, and who wants people to know which school they go to? I certainly wouldn't/didn't. That could seriously cramp your style. On the other hand, the argument against wearing school uniform is that everyone looks like clones, with one individuality – anonymous, in fact. Great! I'm all for that! The last thing you want at school is for anyone to know who you are. If they do, they'll start asking you questions, sending you on errands, and so forth. But if you're anonymous you can be whoever you please: the kid who never gets sent on errands because they always get it wrong, for instance. Oh, yeah! Give me uniform every time!

WINTER SKIRT – EXTRA DOUBLE SCRATCHY SUPER THICK LOW GRADE, PLEASE-DON'T-MAKE-ME-WEAR-IT, WOOL

SOCK (WHITE)

SOCK (BLUE)

WHITE, BLUE OR GREY SHIRT (OR WHITEY-BLUEY-GREY IF IT'S BEEN WASHED TOO MUCH)

1. As opposed to uniform, I mean!

132

SCHOOL PULLOVER-
(AFTER WASHING)

HAT - IF YOUR SCHOOL
HAS HATS THEY MUST
BE AS UGLY AS
POSSIBLE

SOCK
(GREY)

SCHOOL BLAZER
FAR TOO BIG BUT MUM SAYS
YOU'LL GROW INTO IT

TIE -
ANY
DISGUSTING
COLOUR YOU
CAN THINK OF

SENSIBLE
SHOES

SUMMER DRESS-
ADJUST LENTH
ACCORDING TO HEAD
TEACHER'S MORALS

LESS SENSIBLE SHOES

133

HELMET
(FOR CRICKET BALLS
OR BULLIES)
BELONGS TO WAYNE

SOCK
(FOR AVOIDING)
BELONGS TO
KEV

OLD PLASTER

SCHOOL STRIP
(FOR FOOTBALL·
AND LAUGHING AT)
BELONGS TO GARY

CRICKET BOX
(FOR .. AH
.. WELL

OLD
PLASTER

SHORTS — AS
BAGGY AS POSSIBLE
(ALSO FOR LAUGHING AT)
BELONGS TO MACKA

BOOT
(FOR FOOTBALL)
BELONGS TO
DWAYNE

BOOT
(FOR THE LEFT
FOOT BALL)
BELONGS TO
DAVE

SOCK (FOR GASSING
SMALL ANIMALS)
LAST WASHED - 1987
BELONGS TO BAZZA

SWIMMING TRUNKS
BELONGS TO GRANDPA

134

Unions, teaching

You may not realize it, but there are more teaching unions than just the NUT. Yes! Not all teachers are NUTs, just most of them. In fact there are a large number of unions for teachers to belong to. Here are some of them:

The Society of Headteachers
The Deputy Headteachers' Union
The Union of Headteachers Without Deputies
The Union of Deputy Headteachers Who Haven't Got Headteachers, Are Still Waiting For One To Be Appointed, Have Been Doing The Job Themselves For Months Standing On Their Heads, And Have Applied For The Job But Probably Won't Get It Because Of That Business With the Gerbil.

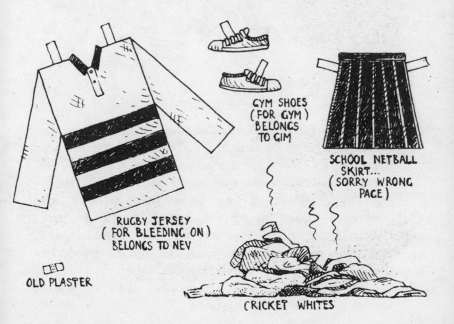

GYM SHOES
(FOR GYM)
BELONGS
TO GIM

SCHOOL NETBALL
SKIRT...
(SORRY WRONG
PAGE)

RUGBY JERSEY
(FOR BLEEDING ON)
BELONGS TO NEV

OLD PLASTER

CRICKET WHITES

V

Verrucas

Yes, they're the scourge of the shower cubicle! And good for a forged note that'll get you out of almost anything, except a trip to the doctor's to have them removed!

W

Waste

In these hard times, when classroom resources are short and there have to be at least 7,000 pupils on the roll for the school to qualify for a pencil, I can see some obvious ways to save enormous amounts of money. Take spelling tests, for instance. The teacher must know which children are going to get the answers wrong, so why bother letting them write anything down, because it's only going to get screwed up, isn't it? Much better to let those children play Gameboy while the clever kids do the test, thus saving whole rainforests of paper. Good idea or what, eh?

X

X-pupils

Don't you just hate them? They turn up at school, get hauled up on the platform during assembly and start going on about how well they're doing, and all because they worked really hard at school. If they're doing as well as they say they are, how come they've got time to talk to you lot?

Y

Youth training schemes

When you finally leave school, if you can't get a job, there's something you can do.[1] You can go on a Youth Training Scheme. These are excellent, and the stuff they teach you is very valuable. So valuable, in fact, that it's amazing no-one thought of teaching it to you while you were still at school.

1. Apart from going on the dole, of course!

Z

Zebra crossing
There are too few of these outside schools. A large number of schools open directly on to main roads, which are a potential hazard. However, help is at hand in the shape of the jolly little Lollipop Person. What a cute figure they cut in their long white plastic mac and peaked cap! I can hardly wait to retire, so that I can become one. But a word of warning: before you put your hand (and your life) into the woolly mittened hand of the Lollipop person, remember: they could be a retired caretaker! You have been warned!

DAY TIME   FULL MOON

Well, that's it, an A–Z of school. I hope you found it useful. If nothing else, it'll help you to learn which letter follows which! However, if used carefully it should provide an indispensable guide to the ins, outs, ups, downs and sidewayses of school life. But keep it to yourself. After all, we don't want the teachers to realize that you can now cope, do we? If they do, they may well be encouraged to devise further, more devious ploys to make your lives miserable. Mind you, if they did that they would just be cutting off their own noses to spite their faces,[1] wouldn't they, because they'd make their lives miserable, too!

1. I don't know whether you're familiar with this old expression. It basically means that you might cut off your own nose to spite, upset, hurt or annoy the rest of your own face. It seems a bit unlikely to me. I can't see your ear – for instance – giving a monkey's whether you've got a nose or not, can you? Your mouth might get a bit fed up, but only because it would have to work a bit harder on the breathing.

Appendix .... .

As promised, I am reprinting the minutes of a meeting of the school governors of a primary school. This is a valuable document, because I think it provides a real insight into the running of a modern school. In these times when money is short and schools are, more and more, being expected to take responsibility for their own future, it's refreshing to see just how well this typical primary school is rising to the challenge. I take my hat off to it, I really do.[1]

Minutes of the meeting of the Governors of the Fitts Bumbly[2] County Primary School, held on the 28th of February, 1993, in the cleaner's cupboard.

Those present:
R. Bisto (Chairperson)
B. Civil (Vice Chairperson)
P. Quickly (Robbery Chairperson)
A. Parsnip (Drugs Chairperson)
A. Plus (Head Teacher)
D. Minus (Rest of Body Teacher)

Governors:
J. Cloth
O. Blymee
Q. Neatly

1. Figuratively speaking, that is. I'm not actually wearing one.
2. Fitts Bumbly was a man of great intelligence (for a Victorian). He was the first British explorer to reach the foot of Mount Everest, look up and say, "If you think I'm climbing that you need your head examining!"

Parent governors:
S. Bend
C. Dee
F.N. Anblindin

Local Education Office observers:
Zippy and George

Also present:
Miss Prim[1]

1) *Minutes of last meeting*
After much discussion, it was decided that the last meeting had gone on for several minutes, hours probably, although no-one could remember much about it.

2) *Matters arising (from last meeting)*
Mrs Neatly asked Mr Dee if he still had that nasty cold he'd had at the last meeting. Mr Dee assured her that it was nearly better. However, the meeting stopped while Mrs Neatly moved her chair as far away from Mr Dee as possible, and everyone gargled with TCP.

3) *Head teacher's report*
The headteacher, Ms Plus, reported that she was still the headteacher, despite attempts by some of the newer staff to oust her in a military coup, using weapons made by boys from the local comprehensive school in their metalwork lesson. She went on to show the governors some shopping she had done that afternoon, while she was meant to be hearing the top juniors read. Mrs Bend complained about this,[2] and Ms Plus pointed out that if they couldn't read by now, they probably never would be able to.[3]

1. Chained to the radiator, as you will remember!
2. This was probably jealousy because she can't get into a size 10 (or a size 20 for that matter)!
3. This proved to be surprisingly accurate.

It was at this point that Miss Prim was overcome by the heat from the radiator, and the meeting was adjourned.[1]

The meeting was reconvened with:

4) *Report of the finance committee*
Mr Quickly, chairman of the finance committee, informed the meeting that he would have to leave early as he had to report to his probation officer. He then submitted his report:

Money in the building fund stood at £90.00.

Money in the emergency fund stood at £00.03p

Mrs Anblindin expressed a view, apparently held by the rest of the governors, that there seemed very little point in having a building fund since the school already had a building, so why bother to save for one? Everyone agreed. Mr Parsnip suggested that the money would be better spent on a Teasmaid. That way they could be woken up at the end of each meeting with a hot drink. This was agreed by everyone except Mr Civil, who was found to be dead.[2] The police were called, and Mr Blymee insisted on putting on a disguise before they entered the building. Since the arrival of the police had rather put everyone off their stroke, and the pubs were open, it was decided to end the meeting in the local. There was the usual singing of the National Anthem, juggling from Miss Minus, and a short recital of *The Songs of Gilbert and Sullivan* from Mr Bisto.

5) It was decided that the meeting should be confidential, as the governors didn't want nosey parents

1. The governors all went behind the bike sheds for a smoke.
2. Actually he had been dead for some weeks, but no-one had noticed.

knowing anything about the running of the school, except the three parent governors who didn't count.[1]

The meeting closed at something past five.[2]

---

1. Or spell.
2. The big hand had fallen off the school clock.